Media
Choices

JEAN MILLS   RICHARD MILLS   LES STRINGER

Oxford University Press 1990

Oxford University Press, Walton Street, Oxford OX2 6DP

Oxford New York Toronto
Delhi Bombay Calcutta Madras Karachi
Petaling Jaya Singapore Hong Kong Tokyo
Nairobi Dar es Salaam Cape Town
Melbourne Auckland

and associated companies in
Beriut Berlin Ibadan Nicosia

Oxford is a trade mark of Oxford University Press

© Jean Mills, Richard Mills, Les Stringer

First published 1990

ISBN 0 19 8311 680

All rights reserved. No part of this publication may be reproduced,
stored in a retrieval system, or transmitted, in any form, or by any means
electronic, mechanical, photocopying, recording, or otherwise, without the
prior permission of Oxford University Press

This book is sold subject to the condition that it shall not, by way of
trade or otherwise, be lent, re-sold, hired or otherwise circulated,
without the publisher's prior consent in any form of binding or cover
other than that in which it is published and without a similar condition
including this condition being imposed on the subsequent purchaser

Typeset by Pentacor Ltd, High Wycombe, Bucks
Printed in *Singapore*

The authors and publishers would like to thank all the teachers who have helped in the
preparation of this book by testing material in 4th and 5th year classes and by suggesting
different approaches. Thanks are due especially to:

Elaine Chant, Cadbury College
Tony Grady, Four Dwellings School
Lorna Ockenden, The Woodrush High School
Ralph Ockenden, Stourport High School
Lynne Woody, Shenley Court School
Ian Wainwright, Queensbridge School

Contents

ADVERTISING

TOWN VIEW	4
SAVE! SAVE! SAVE!	6
THE EAGLE HAS BEEN LANDED	8
FROM DAN DARE TO MOBIL OIL	12
SCRIPT ON AND ON AND ON	14

TELEVISION AND RADIO

BLIND DATE	16
MORE REAL THAN REAL LIFE	20
ARE YOU IN THE PICTURE?	24
ZAP TO THE FUTURE	28
INTERVIEWING AN INTERVIEWER	30
RADIO PLAYS	32
TAKE A LETTER	34
EYE WITNESSES	36

NEWSPAPERS

UNDERGROUND FIRE	38
CHILDREN AT THE GATE	42
SUSPENDED FOR STEALING A KISS	46
PHOTO AND BE DAMNED?	48
SILKWOOD	50

MAGAZINES AND COMICS

MAGAZINE SPOTTING	52
BRIEF ENCOUNTERS	54
RECORD REVIEWS	58
PHOTO-STORY	60
NOT SO COMIC	64

FILM

WHAT'S IN A FILM?	68
THE MAN FROM SNOWY RIVER	70
HOPE AND GLORY	74
STAGECOACH	78
VERY SPECIAL EFFECTS	82

BRIEFING

PEOPLE GRADING	86
LEGAL, DECENT, HONEST AND TRUTHFUL?	88
READING THE SMALL PRINT	92
GOOD NEWS	94
PLANNING A DOCUMENTARY	96
IT'S IN THE SCRIPT	100
WRITING A NEWSPAPER ARTICLE	102
FILM REVIEWS	104
GLOSSARY	108
SKILLS CHECKLIST FOR TEACHERS	110

ADVERTISING

Town View

These photographs were all taken in the West Midlands town of West Bromwich.

A

B

C

D

E

F

1. What does each photo tell you about the area? (You might look at the style and age of the buildings, the range of people, the opportunities for leisure and shopping.)
   What is your overall view of this town from these photographs?

2. Photographs can be cut, with parts left out, so as to present a different message. This is known as cropping. One of the photographs has a red line showing where it could be cropped.
   What is the effect of this cropping?
   How could three of the remaining photographs be cropped so as to present a better or worse view of the town?

3. Select the photos you might use in a brochure which seeks to attract:
   Either: new businesses to the area,
   or: tourists.
   As you do so, keep notes about which pictures you rejected/selected and why.
   Then write the brief explanation that could accompany each of the photos for the particular brochure you have chosen, aiming your words either at business people or tourists.

G

H

Research

Either:
Take some photographs, or produce a five-minute video, of your own area to show what it is like to live there. Present your view to another school or college in one of the following forms:
a an album or display of photos with captions
b a video-recording, with commentary
c a colour-slide programme, with explanation
d a tape-slide sequence, with appropriate music and sound effects.

Or:
Write notes for a company which is to produce a brochure advertising your town or area. Include details of the main attractions for all age groups in the community and explain the places from which some of the best photographs could be taken.

Or:
Interview four or five people in order to produce a report on what they consider attractive or ugly about the area where they live.

ADVERTISING

Save! Save! Save!

Styles in advertising and in photography change over the years. What was attractive and eye-catching in 1935 seems very old-fashioned now. This Unit is about changing tastes and about successful advertising.

1986 was the one hundred and twenty-fifth anniversary of the National Savings movement and there was a major showing around the country of National Savings posters. Here are some of them.

1935

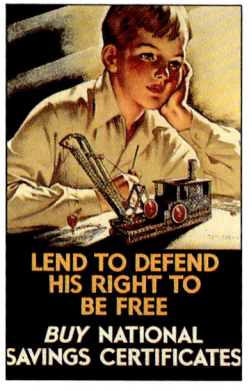
1940

1943

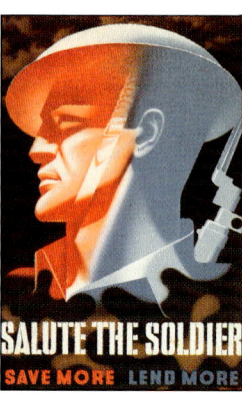
1944

1947

1951

1959

1986

These advertising posters are also historical documents. They show changes in people's lives and attitudes. They show different art techniques over the years.

See if you can spot some of the changes by considering these questions:

1. Each poster tells a mini-story. What is it? (For example, 1951: The family that saves can enjoy a happy summer holiday.)
2. What different themes are shown in each of the war years' posters: 1939–1945? (For example, 1940: Freedom for future generations.)
3. How are the war years' posters different from those of 1947 and 1951?
4. What are the different attitudes shown in these posters towards men and women?
5. In what technical way is the poster of 1986 different from all the others?
6. Which of these posters:
   a do you like best? Why?
   b do you like least? Why?
   c is the best as a work of art? Why?
   d would encourage you to buy National Savings Certificates or Bonds, or put money in the Post Office? Why?

Points of advice

Look now at some points of advice about illustrations from David Ogilvy, who runs an advertising agency with 141 offices in 40 countries.

Point 1 The subject of your illustration is all important. If you don't have a remarkable idea for it, not even a great photographer can save you.

Point 2 The kind of pictures which work best are those which arouse the reader's curiosity.

Point 3 Showing the end result of using your product helps you to sell more.

Point 4 Photographs, rather than drawings, attract more readers, are more believable, and better remembered.

Point 5 Using well-known characters helps viewers to remember the advertisement.

Point 6 Keep your illustrations as simple as possible, with the focus on one person. Crowd scenes don't pull.

Point 7 Don't show human faces enlarged bigger than life size. Readers don't like them.

Point 8 Historical subjects bore most readers.

Point 9 Don't think the topics which interest you will also interest your viewers.

Point 10 Advertisements in four colours cost half as much again as black and white, but, usually, they are twice as memorable. A good bargain.

Complete a copy of the chart below, matching three of the National Savings posters against Ogilvy's points. Use this code:

√ = poster fits point of advice
x = poster does not fit point of advice
o = not relevant

Research

1. Match Ogilvy's points against three other advertisements you see in newspapers and magazines and on hoardings, and report your findings to your group.

2. Produce your own National Savings poster for either one of the missing years or for the year 2000.

	1935	1940	1943	1944	1947	1951	1959	1986
Point 1								
2								
3								
4								
5								
6								
7								
8								
9								
10								

ADVERTISING

The Eagle has been landed

This is the tale of how one man was used by the media.

Eddie: the story so far

AT ABOUT 2pm today a 24-year-old plasterer-cum-babysitter from Cheltenham will climb a 90-metre ski jump tower to resume his quest for a gold medal at the Olympic Games.

As he peers from the top of the chute at Calgary, among his most fervent wishes will be that his glasses do not mist up under his goggles before take-off.

Michael "Eddie" Edwards is a star of the 1988 Winter Olympics.

At the first glimpse of contestant number 24, resplendent in air-force blue and licking the gingery stubble above his upper lip in nervous anticipation, the 50,000-strong crowd roared its approval.

When Eddie saluted his many admirers, having safely executed an appalling 55-metre jump, arms flailing, legs akimbo, looking more like a geriatric turkey than an eagle their cheers doubled. History will record that the plucky Edwards made a second 55-metre jump. This left him comfortably 58th in the 58-man field.

While any other competitor would have been as sick as a parrot at such a performance, Eddie the Eagle later described his experience as "amazing- the crowd was so enthusiastic. This is the best day of my life! Now I'm an Olympic Great!"

The Financial Times

Eddie has his critics

'What more is there to say about this Englishman who's been labelled the best British but the world's worst ski-jumper, the Charlie Chaplin of the winter Olympics, Eddie the Eagle?'

Cliff Morgan. Radio 4.

Eddie has his supporters

NOBODY who has the courage to launch himself off a 70-metre ski jump and travel at 65 miles an hour deserves the kind of shabby treatment you gave Eddie the Hero Edwards. Let's face it, he had the whole world behind him, EXCEPT your reporter.
R. Stinton, Motherwell

I WAS DISGUSTED that your reporter mocked Eddie Edwards' jump at Calgary. How dare you call him a flop? He's shown guts and determination against all odds.
If I was a member of Eddie's family, my heart would be bursting with pride. It is anyway.
Good for you, Eddie!
Wendy Lewis, Bucks

"With every jump, he has slipped increasingly into the role of a clown."
"Where would the Olympic Games go if people like Edwards took their place in every discipline and so discredited the sporting achievements of all those who far outstrip them in ability, yet not so far as to receive victory cheers."

Junge Welt

Already there are murmurings that some British athletes believe the publicity is out of all proportion.

The Guardian

Eddie has his appeal

- 'He's got everything that we want. To get that bit of magic off of him. To feel that spirit in him.'
  (Girl)

- 'Oh, he's a doll. He's a sweetheart.'
  (Girl)

- 'The guy is big, real big. When he comes in tonight, I want to have a chance to talk to him and, er, I don't know what the man is made of, but I want to meet that man.'
  (Male spectator)

- 'Because you can feel happiness when you're all talking about Eddie, Eddie the Eagle, Eddie Edwards, Eddie and the Eaglettes.'
  (Girl)

- 'He's like the next-door neighbour, or a little brother, or a big brother who's doing well, and I feel really pleased for him.'
  (Female spectator)

- 'Every year, every day, the people would like to touch somebody or associate with an ordinary guy. That's no different than the ordinary things that happened to Presley in his small days, or have happened to anybody in this industry. The world creates a star 'cos, inside of every one of us, we'd all like to have a little recognition.'
  (Advertising executive)

- 'I'm not the best jumper by a long way. I will be eventually but I'm not yet. But people still love to come up and get my autograph. And I think that's one of the reasons I'm so popular because the other jumpers don't, erm, they don't take time to, sort of, sign autographs and take photographs with the kids and things like that, whereas I will. And I think the crowd appreciates that.'
  (Eddie)

Eddie has problems

- *Eddie the man, the myth, the legend. The biggest thing out of Britain since the Beatles.* A typical headline here this week and, yes, it's referring to an amiable athlete who finished, comfortably last. But then, this is the West, where they adore pioneers, and a record's being released, dedicated to the spirit of Eddie the Eagle Edwards. But even that's a con. It was written for the Los Angeles Olympics four years ago.

- I'm afraid what began as a harmless wheeze, rather like the skiing, has been blown off course. The problem, you see, is that Canada and the United States only have one bronze medal each from their exploits so far. There's been a major media panic and Edwards has become an innocent pawn. The likeable eagle is now the prey and the vultures are moving in.

- Eddie agreed to attend a Las Vegas star show. He was the guest of honour. And I'm not sure he knew what he was letting himself in for. It was almost as if the Beatles had decided to re-form for the night. The whole evening was completely stage-managed by marketing men who've arrived on the scene now. They've got T-shirts and records and cheerleaders. Eddie was mobbed. He looked bewildered. A week ago, when he arrived here, he was a relaxed sportsman, looking forward to his Olympics. And last night he looked frightened, stunned, out of his depth, rather like a fish gasping for air.

- The eagle, remember, is supposed to be an endangered species. This one should have been protected, from outrageous exploitation.

Radio commentators

The story is about how media experts take up an unknown person and use him for their own purposes.

1. Read through the extracts and tell the story of Eddie to a partner who asks you questions about him.

2. Eddie's appeal is compared to that of pop stars. How is it the same/different?

3. What are some of Eddie's problems?

4. Are you one of his supporters or critics? Why?

5. The story of Eddie raises questions, such as:
   a. Is it right to use a person in this way to sell products?
   b. Is it fair that Eddie, who comes last in the ski-jump, gets more publicity than the winner?
   c. Is it fair to make him a figure of fun when, in fact, he is a serious athlete?
   d. To what extent was Eddie a willing partner in the publicity craze?

   List all the arguments either condemning or supporting the use of Eddie by the media. Then use your list in discussion with a partner who takes the opposite view.

6. Several companies seem to want Eddie to advertise their products. Choose one product and explain how Eddie could be used in a TV advertisement for the company. Write an account of the advert which includes details of:
   - location (where the action is set)
   - action (what actually happens)
   - narrative (the *story* of the advert)
   - dialogue (who says what)
   - background music and/or sound effects
   - impact (the particular idea or incident which people should remember and connect with the product)

7. Write a fantasy story in which you are taken up and promoted by an advertising agency.

Eddie has a future?

There are various rumours about Eddie:
- that he's been made a life member of the Monster Raving Loony Party who want him to practise on the European butter mountain;
- that a well-known sports firm is chasing him to advertise their goods in a roadshow;
- that he's received hefty offers from firms representing vodka, tobacco and cameras;
- that Eddie intends to spend his advertising money on training and equipment so as to become a serious Olympic contender.

Since the Games began, Eddie has been approached by promoters of goods, ranging from cigars to four-wheel drive vehicles, anxious for the budding celebrity's endorsement of their products. If he plays his cards right, the Eagle's distinctive features may beam out of TV sets during many a commercial break. After his courageous but comical attempts to survive two more 90-metre leaps into the unknown today, the last laugh may well be his.

The Financial Times

The whole comic issue about the poor fellow is getting out of hand and there is some feeling that the press who helped create him are now poised to destroy him. Let's hope his career does not finish painfully.

The Sunday Times

ADVERTISING

From Dan Dare to Mobil Oil

What do advertisers aim to do when they promote a product?

This is what one advertising agency, Gold, Greenlees and Trott (GGT), says:

For most people, advertising is about as important as putting the milk bottle out at night. It's a mistake to believe that people are out there, waiting for our next message.

Impact is our first priority. We set out to produce advertising which gets noticed and which demands attention.

This is closely followed by relevance. This means that all our advertising, like pearls, should be created around a piece of grit. This is a single-minded idea which comes from the product (such as, 'Most of the sugar turns to alcohol', in the Holsten Pils lager campaign).

Finally, it's very important that people remember what the advertisement was for in the first place, so that they don't confuse similar products.

1. This statement is in four paragraphs. Each paragraph makes one main point. Try to represent the four points as a labelled diagram which would explain them simply and clearly. Explain your diagram to a partner.

A company like GGT uses as many as ten teams to work on a campaign. Teams are made up of an Art Director and a Copy Writer. The Art Director provides the visual ideas; the Copy Writer does the writing. A brief summary like the one that now follows, is produced by each team for each idea.

2. Here are four examples of advertisements from GGT. Copy out the brief summary and complete it for each advertisement.

3. a What is there in each of these pictures which sticks in your mind?
   b Which two are from magazines and which two are from posters? How can you be sure?
   c Each of the adverts has a slogan which would be repeated time and again. What are they? Which is the best and why?

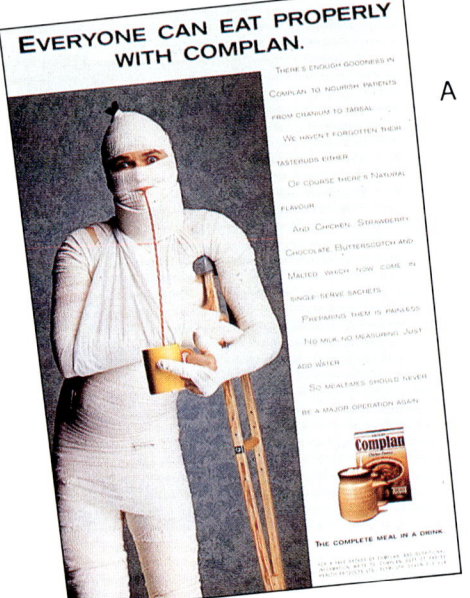

A

B

Brief Summary

Client ....
Product ....

What job is this ad trying to do? ....
....

What should they think when they see it? ....
....

What problems do we face with this product? ....
....

Brand Images

GGT says, 'It's very important that people remember what the advertisement was for in the first place, so that they don't confuse similar products.' This is part of the idea behind *brand images* or *branding*.

For example, TV adverts for Mobil Oil featured the spaceman Dan Dare from the old *Eagle* comic. The adverts scored very highly for impact, but research later discovered that, while most viewers (80%) could remember the adverts, only a few (4%) knew they were about Mobil fuels.

The other part of branding means that the advertisers give the product a personality. For example, the brand image of Volvo cars is that they are solid, strongly built, reliable and safe. The brand image of Fairy Liquid is to do with a caring person who uses a caring product on delicate skin.

1. What kind of brand image is GGT trying to give:
    Complan (A)
    Farley's Rusks (B)
    Morrisons (C)
    Honeywell (D).

2. Design another advert (either for a magazine or poster) for one of these products, trying to keep to the same brand image. Ask three of your classmates to judge your success.

Research

1. Choose three adverts from a magazine. Say briefly how each advert makes its impact and how good you think it is. Compare your views with a partner's.

2. Choose three TV adverts. Say what the brand image is of each product and explain how the advert builds it up.

3. Using material from this unit, but with your own examples, write a report entitled *Brand Image* to explain the idea to someone who has never met it before. Remember to comment on the part played by **Impact, Slogan** and **Personality,** in building up a brand image.

ADVERTISING

Script On and On and On

Here is part of the script for an Ariston dishwasher TV commercial.

Client: Ariston **Product:** Dishwasher/Fridge-freezer	**Title:** Hokusai **Length:** 30 secs.
Visuals	**Sound-track**
Everything in the foreground is 3D stop frame animation. The background is a 2D painting. Open on a Hokusai (i.e. Japanese artist) 'wave' scene with an Ariston dishwasher in the foreground. Waves break in the background. Amongst them pots, pans and cutlery are being tossed around. Next to the dishwasher a pair of saucers animate like lips to sing the words. 2 cups roll in to form eyes. Pans roll in to form a body. Cut to 'ARISTON'. The words 'ON & ON & ON & ON' appear after it, filling the screen.	Music: Sung to 'Da Da Da' Trio. 'When you buy an Ariston, its guarantee is five years long, lasts well past 1991. ARISTON and on and on and on.'

1 Discuss the script with a partner and make notes on some of the technical terms, to explain their meaning:
   a foreground   b 3D
   c 2D   d open on
   e cut to

2 Each part of the advert is doing a different job and should have a different effect on the viewer. What, then, should viewers think:
   a when they see the animation?
   b when they hear the music?
   c when they see the logo ARISTON?
   d when they hear the voice-over commentary?

3 Look again at the words in the Visuals section of the Ariston script. Making only a few changes, turn them into a free verse poem.

4 Here is a checklist by a professional advertiser, David Ogilvy, on how to write good TV commercials.

a Brand identification. Use the name within the first ten seconds or viewers will remember the commercial but forget the product. Play games with the name.

b You have only 30 seconds. If you grab attention straightaway you stand a better chance of holding the viewer.

c When you have nothing to say, sing it.

d Voice-over or on-camera. It's harder to hold your audience if you use voice-over. It's better for actors to talk on-camera.

e It pays to reinforce your message by having the voice-over speak the words as they are shown on the screen.

f Show the viewers something they have never seen before. An average family has the TV on for six hours a day and sees around 30,000 commercials a year. Make your commercial different.

g Don't change the scene too often; viewers get confused.

h The same idea can be used over a long period. It helps to give a brand image and reminds people of your product (for example, the Esso tiger).

i Show the product in use.

j Everything is possible on TV. The technicians can produce anything you want. The only limit is your imagination.

k Make your commercials crystal clear or they will be misunderstood by the public.

Choose five items from this list that you think have been used to good effect in the Ariston advert. Put them in order of priority, with the most important first.

5 Write the script to go with the London Docklands advert aimed at business people. You can add more visuals if you want to. Use the Ariston example and Ogilvy advice as guides. The main idea you need to work into your commercial is given to you.

a **London Docklands**   'Why move to the middle of nowhere when you can move to the middle of London?'

6 Now you have written your own commercial, add two or three more points of advice to the check list, based on your own experience.

Research

1 Look carefully at a video of any commercial which you like. Match it against the ten advice points and write a report for your group (or for the company itself) on how closely it seems to follow that advice.

2 Many commercials tell a story. For example, for over twenty years Oxo adverts have shown us a family. Others show a particular incident or adventure or, in the case of Hovis, go back in time.
Try to track this story-line by studying commercials and making brief notes on the story-line of three of them. To do this, you might use sections such as:

Product being advertised ....
....
Characters ....
....
....
Location ....
....
....
....
Action and Dialogue ....
....
....
....
....

Tell your partner the story of one commercial, detail by detail.

TELEVISION AND RADIO

Blind Date

Blind Date is a television game show watched by millions. The aim of the show is for one contestant to choose another to take on a blind date. He or she (known as the *pickers*) questions three members of the opposite sex (known as *pickees*) who are hidden behind a screen, and makes a choice. They are then introduced to each other by the show's presenter. A few days later they go on their date, which might be at home or abroad. A photographer goes with them and, the following week, viewers see film of the date and hear what happened.
Read on and discover the different stages the show goes through before viewers see it.

Stage 1: **Selection**

Contestants for *Blind Date* are carefully chosen in the first place. People who want to be on the show write in. The applications are sorted and possible contestants are chosen. Then an interviewer phones and arranges to talk to them.

Stage 2: **Pickers and pickees**

After auditions some are chosen to be pickers (choosers) or pickees (those who are chosen).
In choosing contestants, the production team tries to:
a   select people from different parts of the country and who do different jobs;
b   match a picker and a pickee who might get on well together;
c   match people by age;
d   look for those who have a good personality for television.

Try this for yourself.
Here are descriptions of eight possible contestants. Choose one picker (male or female) and three pickees (three males or three females) for a future show.

Lou, from Glasgow.
Air Steward.
Age 27.

Has been called a show-off.
Lively and confident.
Very quick in auditions to answer the questions.

Beverley, from Cardiff.
Waitress.
Age 24.

Did some very funny impersonations at the audition.
Rather a smart dresser.
A forceful personality.

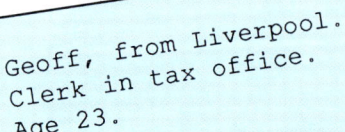

Geoff, from Liverpool.
Clerk in tax office.
Age 23.

Very observant, especially of other people. Can see behind the front which people put up.
Speaks slowly and clearly.
Appears steady and dependable.

Jane, from Belfast.
Computer programmer.
Age 21.

Very bubbly personality.
Sometimes talks without listening to others.   Good humoured.
Pushy.

Debbie, from Chester.
Unemployed.
Age 20.

Appeared to be too serious at first, until you realise she's actually taking the mickey out of the show with her wise-cracks. Pretty brainy.

Martin, from Luton.
Works in a wine bar.
Age 20.

Easy-going and described as very good company. Talkative but polite and well-mannered. Has a permanent limp from a childhood accident.

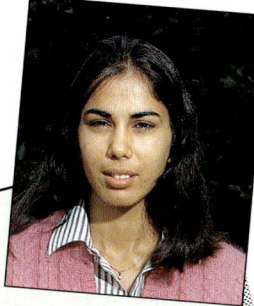

Sarah, from Kent.
Air hostess.
Age 24.

Good sense of humour and quick-witted. Puts herself out to help others. Can she stand up for herself?

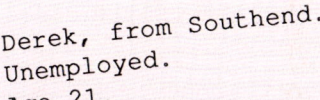

Derek, from Southend.
Unemployed.
Age 21.

Rather cautious but prepared to make fun of himself. Sensitive but covers this up with smart answers.

Stage 3: **Show on air**

The show is nearly ready to be put on. The presenter (here Cilla Black) describes her final preparations.

I get the script three days before the studio usually, and then I come in, say, the day before the studio for what we laughingly call the 'read through'. Sometimes we waste half an hour gossiping about what happened to me last week, and I'm apologising for not having watched the 'bish-bash'. The 'bish-bash', as we call it, means the bit when a couple have been on the date and they come back and are filmed, and we find out what they said about each other. I get a tape of that with the script, and I try to look at it before I go to the read through, so that I can work out my own questions for the couples coming back. Of course, some questions are sorted out for me which, with the script, I put in my own words.

We watch the bish-bashes, go through the script, and read the biographies of the Numbers 1s, 2s and 3s etc., and we all muck in – and out of it I get a lot of ideas. But I really can't script my answers, so what you see is what you get!

It's an easy day for me, the preparation day, but the studio day, that's different, particularly if it's on a Monday. I hate doing *Blind Date* on a Monday, because my Nanny doesn't come back to work on a Monday until after the kids have gone back to school, so I'm up at the crack of dawn, half past six or whatever. If the studio is on any other day, it's different, because I like a good eight hours' sleep, so I don't get up until about nine o'clock, do my hair, 'cos I always do my own hair for *Blind Date*, and then have a brunch. At about 1.30 pm, LWT very kindly send a car for me and Bobby (Cilla's husband) 'cos I'm due on the studio floor at 2.30 in the afternoon.

I do a very quick rehearsal, really it's just for cameras, sound and lighting, and actually I'm not very good at rehearsals. I don't rehearse with the actual kids who are going to be on, I rehearse with actors and actresses pretending to be them. Then I go to my dressing room, and go over my script and the biographies again, and try and remember everyone's name.

After an hour or so, I do go and meet the pickers. We do two shows a night, and I don't meet the rest of the kids until the show, but the pickers are hidden away and can't obviously meet the people they will be going on a date with, so I have a little chat and welcome them to the studio. Once they're all relaxed, I go and get my polyfilla on . . . I go to make-up! That's usually around 4.30 pm, and after I've got that on, I go back to the dressing room, and I literally interview Bobby. He plays all the parts, and I don't know what I'd do without him. I interview him like he's been on the date, and he's really very good.

After I've done all that, I have a light supper and then all of a sudden it's 'check make-up' time, and I change into whatever I'm wearing for the show. Once I'm dressed and ready to go, Bill Martin, our warm-up man, introduces me to the audience and I go on and have a little chat, and sometimes there's somebody in the audience who'll talk to me, and I love it when the audience talks back because it sort of relaxes me. But once I get on the floor, I wanna get on with it, because it's been a long day – I've taken the kids to school, and now I wanna get the show on the road.

1. How is Cilla's preparation day different from her studio day? Work out her schedule for the studio day and set it out, with times shown. Then add snippets of advice to her as if you were her personal assistant.

2. Which jobs are done by Cilla and which by other people?

3. How can you tell that these are Cilla's spoken words and not a written description?

4. What have you learnt about her from this extract which makes Cilla good at her job?

Timetable

Here is a timetable for a pickee and a picker.

```
Pickee
2.30 p.m.       Briefing
3.00 - 3.45 p.m.    Rehearsal
4.00 p.m.       Practice games
6.30 - 6.45 p.m.    Dressing room - change
6.45 p.m.       Make-up
7.25 p.m.       Taken to studio and hidden.

Picker
4.00 p.m.       Briefing
4.45 - 5.45 p.m.    Rehearsal
5.45 - 6.00 p.m.    Dressing room- change
6.00 p.m.       Practice games
6.45 p.m.       Make-up
7.30 p.m.       Brought from make-up room
```

1. What differences do you notice between these two timetables? What are the reasons for these differences? How are they both different from the presenter's timetable?

2. Choose one of the periods in the contestants' timetable and write out the thoughts that go through the head of a picker or a pickee during that period.

Advice for pickers

1 Always make clear which pickee you are speaking to. Identify them by number. Make sure they speak up and understand the questions.
2 Try to form a picture of each pickee from their first answer. This will help you tell them apart later.
3 Follow up their answers if you want to know more. Have fun with the presenter. Ideally the two of you should be a double act, bouncing off each other (literally if you must!)
4 When you make your choice, say why and make it clear who you are choosing. Don't change your mind.
5 The audience is liable to shriek after you have made your choice. Don't be unnerved or have second thoughts.

Using this advice as a guide, make a list of do's and don'ts for pickees, concentrating on:
- how to speak
- how to show personality
- how to react to other pickees
- how to react to the presenter
- how to behave in front of the camera
- how to react to the audience

Questions

Pickers are asked to make a list of ten questions they might ask. Before the show the producer reduces this list to three questions. Here are a few which have been asked on the show:

a What sort of person would you most want me *not* to be?
b Who is your favourite fictional character and why?
c If you stood in front of a full-length mirror, what nickname would you give yourself?
d I have to confess that I sometimes lie about my age. What do you lie about?
e The last time you had a row, what was it about?
f If you were writing an advertising slogan for yourself, what would it be?

First, try answering these yourself and then, with a partner, make a list of ten questions which you think might help to reveal a contestant's personality. Which are your best three questions?

Research

1 Do a survey of six game shows currently on television and complete this table. The first one is done for you.

	1	2	3
Name of show	Tarby's Frame Game		
Name of presenter	Jimmy Tarbuck		
TV channel	I.T.V.		
Day & time shown	Saturday 7.30 p.m.		
Duration	30 mins		
Appeal of audience	Fast-moving with fabulous prizes.		

Using information from your completed table, present a report for your group on:
- the types of presenters;
- the appeal of game shows.

Or, present a report on how ordinary people are required to behave on game shows, answering these questions:
- How does the host treat the contestants?
- Are the contestants made fun of?
- Are the private lives of contestants made public?
- Should ordinary people be used in these ways for mass entertainment?

TELEVISION AND RADIO

More Real than Real Life

Many people like to talk about their favourite programmes, especially soap operas. They seem hooked on them. In this Unit you can read what people say about soaps and can judge for yourself the appeal of these programmes.

A

Deb (32): You're talking about them as though they're real people.

Dawn (27): Yes, I know. Isn't it awful?

Deb: But this is it, you do, we do. They are part of your life.

Jill (38): Like my husband a little while ago, he said, 'I'm so worried about Benny [from *Crossroads*], I haven't seen him lately.' And for a moment I could see him wondering if he should go and look for him.

Jean (44): Yes, I was on the phone a couple of months ago, I'll never forget this, talking to my friend about this person who'd died on a programme. And when I'd finished my husband said, 'Who died? What happened?' He was really concerned. When I said, 'Oh, whatsisname on whatsisname programme', he – well, he just died laughing. Because, he said, 'I really thought from the way you were talking it was a real person.'

Alice (35): But you do get involved. I was watching *Sons and Daughters* and there was a bit where a very young wife goes out and leaves her little baby. She goes out, and suddenly it's all on its own. I'm going, 'Lyn, please don't', 'They're going to go mad', 'Wait till thing finds out' [*all laughing*] 'He'll go mad . . . the baby . . . her husband . . . Oh, he'll go spare . . .' You know, and I thought, it's only a programme. *There's a camera in front of all that.*

'I identify with the characters, basically. There's one girl called Zoe who's very loud, and very vivacious - just like me. She bowls everybody over with her personality, but she just goes on and on. I can really understand how she feels when people tell her to just shut up.'

Any sort of social problem you can think of, or that you're ever likely to face comes up in *Neighbours* - like teenage pregnancy, couples eloping together, divorces, one woman trying to shoot her husband, that sort of thing. It helps me solve my own problems by showing me the likely outcome of different courses of action. Sometimes it shows you what not to do.

' Only last week this friend of mine, who was desperate to take this girl out, asked me for some advice. It was just like a situation from *Neighbours*, and I thought to myself, 'Well, what did they do?' The only problem was that what they'd done hadn't worked. But I advised my friend to do it anyway, and you know what - it didn't work for them either. Wow!'

'I get upset if I miss *Neighbours* because I'm really hooked on it, you get a little bit every day. With *Dallas* or *EastEnders* you've lost interest between episodes - but when you've got it continually coming at you - Wow! It's magic.'

B Stephanie

C

Alan (37): Well, Ken and Deirdre, when they were having that bust-up, that was so emotional. It was very good TV. It choked you up a bit.

John (44): It was saddest, though, when she went back to him.

Alan: Yes.

John: Yes, I reckon she should have left him.

Dennis (49): I sometimes get sad about Hilda. She gets put upon. Sometimes Hilda gets put upon.

Dennis: I must be perfectly honest, I watched it when Stan died, I watched it and I cried. I sat down and watched it when Stan died, because it was so real and I could relate to it. I just sat there and cried.

D

Maureen (39): I would like her own children to see her for what she really is, especially Steven.

Edna (42): Yes.

Maureen: I would like him to see through her and know what she's done. And then he could say, 'Well, she is still my mother, and I'm still going to love her, but now I know what she is like and in future I'm not going to trust her.' Because she does terrible things, and they find out, and in the next breath she says, 'Oh, but it wasn't me, why do you always think it's me?' And then they say, 'Well, perhaps it wasn't her this time.' I would like them to see through her. Just once.

E

Maureen (39): I mean, in all honesty, if I was a man I wouldn't want her to be my wife, she looks too tarty.

Pat (47): Yes, she is very tarty.

Anne (45): I wish she'd change.

Maureen: I don't think she can now. She's been like that too long.

Pat: The fringe on her forehead.

Maureen: Yes, her hairstyle is so old-fashioned, but I suppose they've got to give that impression.

Molly (41): She's been very unlucky.

Edna (42): Every man she's had has more or less finished with her.

Molly: But that's the part she's meant to play.

Janet (32): The men use her.

Molly: She's been very hurt. I mean when she was with Mike Baldwin she really idolised him, didn't she?

Jean (42): Every time a new man comes along you expect her to start getting off with him.

Anne: Diving in.

1 Which soap operas, past and present, are being discussed in each of these conversations: Describe each of them briefly (or three others you know well) by completing a copy of this chart.

	A	B	E
Title			
Main Characters (4)			
Main Setting			
Recent Events (3)			

2 For each conversation (lettered **A–E**) decide what it is about the soap that appeals to these viewers. Here are some possibilities:
   a There are characters whose lives are a mess and who need help.
   b Some characters are exciting or attractive.

3 Both men and women are discussing these soap operas. Does there seem to be a difference in what attracts men and what attracts women?

4 Most of the speakers are middle-aged. Are their views the same as yours or different? Does Stephanie say anything different from the others?

Gentle lad who charmed a lady

The twenty-five year old soap opera *Crossroads* came to an end in April 1988. One of its best-loved characters was undoubtedly Benny, played by Paul Henry.

For more than twelve years *Crossroads* fans followed with affection the life of gentle, simple-minded Benny.

It was while he was a casual worker at a local farm that he first met Diane Hunter (Susan Hanson). At first alarmed by him she gradually warmed to his childlike nature and set out to help him.

Here are some other episodes from his life.

1
When Benny's grandmother died in 1976, he moved to King's Oak to be closer to his 'Miss Diane'. There, he met Maureen Flynn, and for the first time in his life fell in love. He proposed and, to everyone's amazement, she accepted, recognising that his loyal, steadfast nature would make him an ideal husband. They planned to marry at Christmas 1977, but on the morning of the wedding Maureen was knocked down and killed by a car. Benny never really recovered from the tragedy.

2
Shortly after Benny's arrival at the farm, a man named Tom Reed turned out to be his father and, for a while, Benny went to live at Reed's house with the rest of his family. But they didn't take to him and the arrangement soon fell through.

3
In 1980 Benny was accused of killing farmworker Linda Welsh (left), who - during a violent row with her boyfriend - was pushed to the floor and hit her head. She died instantly and Benny was implicated when the girl's lover told the police that it was Benny who had been arguing with her.

4

Benny spent much of his time doing odd jobs at the garage and on the farm, and occasionally helping out at the motel. But in 1986, he again tangled with the police. This time, when he found some schoolboys tormenting his dog, Moses, he accidently injured the gang's ringleader while rescuing the pet. The boy complained to the police and the outcome was that Benny was remanded for a medical report. Benny was saved when Diane offered legal responsibility for him, as his next-of-kin.

5

In April 1987 Benny's world fell apart when he suffered the cruellest blow of all. 'Miss Diane' suddenly collapsed and was rushed to hospital. But it was too late - she died of a brain haemorrhage. Benny has never got over her death and still mourns his best friend.

1 What do the various episodes in Benny's life-story have in common?

2 From the evidence here say what you think made Benny a popular character.

3 Write a brief biography of a character you admire in a soap opera, along similar lines to this, as if for a TV magazine.

Research

1 Often characters have to be written out of a series or written into one. First, list the ways in which this can be done (for example, by moving away from/into the area). Then choose an existing character in a current soap opera and write an outline to show how that person will leave the series and how the other characters will adjust to the changes.

2 Collect newspaper and magazine stories about a current soap opera. Then write a short story based on one of the characters or incidents.

3 Video some extracts from soap operas and discuss them in your group, saying:
- where events normally take place;
- what group of people the soap is based on;
- what dramatic events happen to the characters;
- what the appeal of the soap is for viewers.

TELEVISION AND RADIO

Are You in the Picture?

How fair is television to all the different groups in our society? This Unit looks at how some old people, black and Asian people and women think they are presented on television. Are they shown true to life or is the picture distorted?

Old People

These statements were made by:

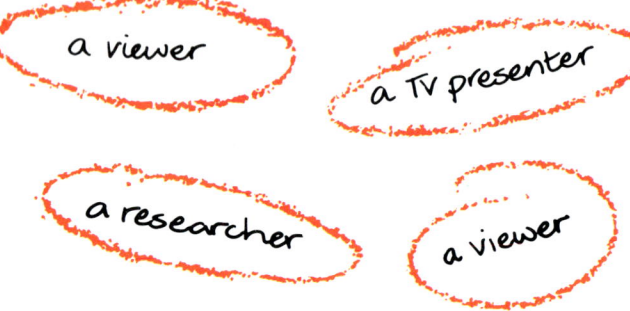

a viewer

a TV presenter

a researcher

a viewer

A The allegation tonight is that ten million people are being stereotyped by television which portrays them as boring, feeble, complaining, mean and utterly sexless. You are one of that ten million if you're over sixty.

B I said to my next-door neighbour one time 'Well, I won't see you for a couple of days, but no dashing about in the meantime.' And she said, 'Oh, well, that's lovely of you to say because I don't dash about any more, but in my dreams I run.' And I thought that was very sweet. She's 91.

C You don't think of yourself as getting old, but you look at other people, or friends of the same generation, and you think, 'Oh, they're getting old, they're old.' But you don't think of yourself as being the same way.

D I think we grow up from the very beginning of our lives in a very graded, age-divided society. If you're at the younger age, it's always better to be older. Once you get beyond forty, forty-five, there's a lot of pressure to wish that you were younger. What it does is disconnect people from the age they are when they are that age, so that in a way, we're only half-alive, we're only half ourselves at any particular stage in our lives.

1 Match the people to the statements.

2 Discuss each statement in pairs, with Partner A defending the comment and Partner B attacking it.

3 Name some old people in regular TV programmes who fit the stereotype mentioned in **A** and some old people who do not. Which group is bigger?

4 How old is an old person? How do old people appear to you in the real world?

Black and Asian People

These statements were made by:

an Asian actress

a black female viewer

a TV editor and presenter

an Asian writer and critic

a black actress

A I've lost count of the number of parts I've been offered which are to do with Indian girls running away from arranged marriages. It gets really boring after a while. Most of the writers are white and they see the Asian community in a certain way and therefore they see the parts you play as stereotyped parts.

B As a mother, I do not see enough images to reflect myself, my husband, my children.

C The first few programmes of *Network East* have bitterly disappointed the Asian community. There is nothing Asian about this programme. The presenters are not representative of the Asians. One of the presenters is, in fact, more English than the English. She could not even pronounce some of the Hindustani names of Indian films. Her accent and delivery are most amusing.

D Soaps have great influence on our attitudes. *EastEnders* is the only one to cast several black actors in leading roles and treat them in an unpatronising manner. Why don't we see more black people on popular programmes?

E When people think of television they tend to think of drama or soap operas, but you're forgetting advertisements, sports commentators, news reports. Black people are fairly invisible unless people in drama want a story-line about a black problem or an Asian problem and then we kind of appear in a clump and are sent away again.

1 Match the people to the statements.

2 Discuss each statement in pairs, with Partner A defending the comment and Partner B attacking it.

3 How do you think black and Asian people are presented on TV? Mention particular programmes and advertisements in which they appear.

4 What are the arguments for having more black and Asian people on TV?

Women

These seven statements were made by:

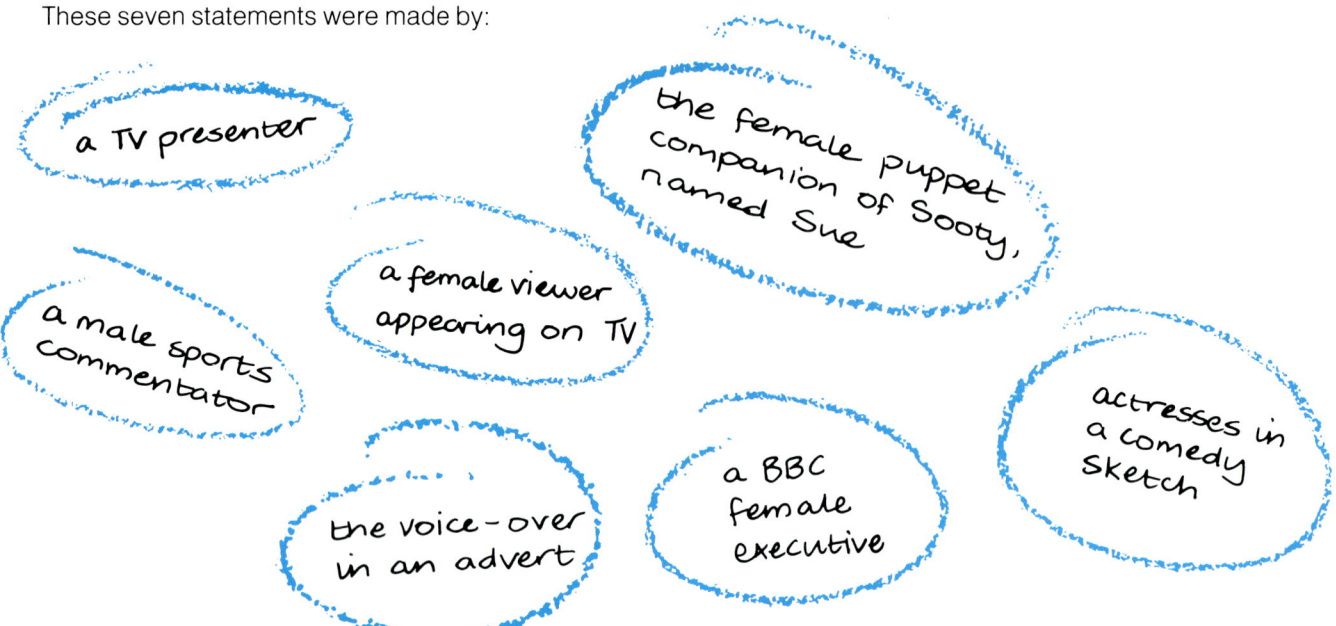

A For him, the latest in do-it-yourself power tools and for her, the latest computerized sewing-machine.

B That's typical of boys, playing hide-and-seek indeed, ha ha! There are more important things to do, like making oneself look beautiful.

C In any week's viewing, the men on screen outnumber the women by about two to one. Things are no better when it comes to presenters. The ratio's still about two to one. And there are even fewer women used as narrators. Only one woman to every eight men.
Sport on television has remained very much a male preserve. In one week sixty hours of sports were shown on television, only four of them featured any women at all.
When it comes to election coverage, there's almost a complete absence of women.

D My response on the telephone was, 'But I'm not at all televisual, because I'm the opposite of what you see on television. I'm not blonde. I haven't got long legs. I'm not young. And I'm certainly not slim. Women always have to look nice on telly. Yet, the men can look slobs.'

E Victoria Wood (V.W.)
Julie Walters (J.W.)
J.W. Did you watch the *News* last night?
V.W. Oh, the nine o'clock?
J.W. Nasty blouse, ugh!
V.W. Quite. We stayed up for *News at Ten*. Three bangles and a polo-neck, thank you!
J.W. Oh no! Her ears are in the wrong place for a polo-neck.

F We still have a letter from a senior executive at the BBC at the time (1970s) saying, 'Women cannot read the News, because if a woman reads the News, no-one will believe the News.'

G Judy has rarely jumped better even in these difficult conditions. I bet she took about four hours to do that hair this morning.

1 Match the people to the statements.

2 Discuss each statement in pairs, with Partner A defending the comment and Partner B attacking it.

3 Which of these speakers seems the most bitter or angry?

4 How do you believe women are presented on TV? Think particularly about:
   a situation comedies
   b the news
   c sport
   d game shows
   e pop music shows

5 All three groups – old people, black and Asian people, women – have at least three things in common. They claim:
  b they lack accurate representation of their point of view;
  c they are shown as stereotypes.
Which statements from each of the three groups can you match together as making similar points about:
  a power
  b representation
  c stereotyping

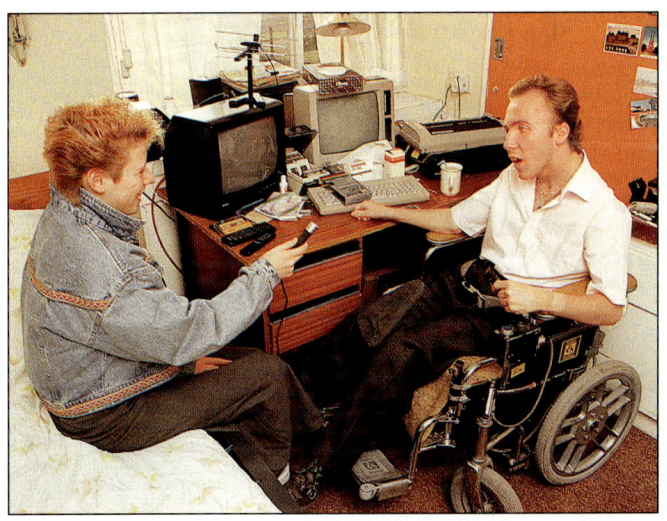

Research

1 How do you think the following groups appear on TV in terms of numbers and presentation:
  a teenagers
  b young children
  c men
  d disabled people
Interview some people from any one of these groups. Tape-record their comments about their presentation on TV and transcribe them. Present an oral or written report on your findings and say what you learned in the process.

2 Set up a chat show programme with yourself as presenter and, either three or four other people, or your class, as a large studio audience, to consider one or two of the issues in this Unit concerned with how people see themselves presented on TV.

3 After watching a particular series or programme or news item, write a letter to the producer about the representation of a group of people which, you felt, was not accurate. Explain what you believe was wrong and say how you think it could be put right in future.

TELEVISION AND RADIO

Zap to the Future

Journalist Alan Rusbridger samples twenty-four hours of satellite TV from a London hotel, room 664.

I checked into the room, ordered some tea and switched on. Room Service eventually arrived, glanced around the room and said: 'Is Sir not watching the football'

Sir was not watching the football.

I was tuned into the Speedway Match of the Week.

Great action from the Swedish Elite League, it said in the programme notes.

The idea was to spurn the traditional four channels for 24 hours and sample the other sources. Get some idea of the satellite and cable revolution. Peer into the future. I did my shift in room 664 of the Grosvenor House Hotel in Park Lane. I wanted to do it at home, but it is not so easy. You have to have a south-facing garden, which I don't. You're also supposed to have planning permission. It seemed a lot of trouble for a day's viewing. The hotel takes 13 channels off Westminster Cable, which plucks them out of the sky. Which was how I ended up in room 664 watching Swedish speedway on Screen Sport (SS).

Time to move on. Zap. An American quiz show. Zap. The Italian weather forecast read in Italian by an Italian in an air steward's uniform. Zap zap. The House of Lords live from Westminster, England. Kansas City versus Oaklaw at baseball. An Arabic soap opera. A vaguely familiar face eating ice-cream. Zap.

Screen Sport is bringing us the Winston Cup Budweiser 500 from Dover. Dover, Kent? Dover, Australia? Dover, New Hampshire? Zap. The Arts Channel has a Czech ballet in which dancers frolic among statues to a backing of Eine Kleine Nachtmusick. Zap.

The ads are confusing. Here's one for Marmite in English, but with a Dutch copyline at the end. And here's one for Ariel with a Belgian housewife dubbed in English. And here's Colgate in English, but with a Dutch accent: 'Fight der build-up on der teeth.' In Dover (Dover, Delaware, it transpires) they have reached lap 351. I dally for a while with Worldnet (WNT), which is run by the US State Department, and take in the 7.30 Times Headline News, read out by a man with a moustache on Sky.

In Dover, Delaware, the race is over. It is time for 10-pin bowling from Toledo, Ohio.

Or perhaps tennis? 'Welcome to a bright and breezy afternoon in Birmingham, England, for live tennis.' *Live* tennis? It seems to be 9.45 pm. Outside the windows of room 664, night is settling over London, England. An American voice takes over. 'What a glorious afternoon. Californian blue skies overhead. Not a cloud in sight.' I order a club sandwich and beer and switch over to the motor racing on Superchannel. One is taking place in Dijon, France, but at this distance I could not tell you which was which.

I resolve to stick with Sky, because they have Carlsberg Euro Football ahead, and also Roving Report on (1) Locusts in Africa; (2) Catfish in Thailand (3) Animal medicine in Los Angeles and (4) Crocodile farms in Australia.

Italian television is showing water polo. I fall asleep in front of American wrestling. 'Just look at that. Awesome! 1,200 pounds of humanity.'

The phone. 'Your 5.25 alarm call, Sir.' Of course. It is time for Good Morning Scandinavia! Or God Morgond Scandinavia!

A Colgate ad in Swedish and then aerobics with Frickis Svettiis, Sweden's answer to the Green Goddess. 'Drrrumm... Draaa... Driggen Ooorskeleken...Ya Skreekkk, Skreekk...ooooh' Or words to that effect.

I order coffee while learning how to make a strawberry and ham salad and improve false nail manicure. Zap.

Europe awakes. Italian breakfast TV is underway. The Music Channel (MTV) is pumping out the first videos of the day. The Children's Channel (CC) is putting out the first animated puppets.

Superchannel (SPC) is telling us how to renovate antique furniture. Arts Channel (AC) has a short feature on the Tower of Babel. 'The World,' says an advert on CNN, 'has become one big neighbourhood.'

Zap. One big neighbourhood. You can now do aerobics from Italy or with an American from London. Sky has a cartoon with a pink mouse. CC has a cartoon with a mauve dog. Super has a cartoon with a green monster.

Zap. A soap opera about a New Zealand country doctor. Zap. An American game show. Zap. My Little Pony.

Lunchtime and LFS has an American courtroom series re-enacting real-life divorce cases in front of a real-life Los Angeles judge. At the end, 'Judge William Keene separates more unhappy couples next week.'

Early afternoon Rugby League from Down Under. Parmatta beat Balmain 32 - 4. It is not quite clear when.

There is Arabic Football on the Arabic channel.

Zap. The House of Lords is back in session. Arts Channel is repeating The Tower of Babel. I have missed A Look at the Ostrich on Super.

A pop presenter is reading a postcard out from a viewer in Portugal. 'I love satellite TV,' it reads 'because it brings some interest into my boring, boring life.' I tiptoe out of my room, downstairs, blinking into the midday afternoon London sun.

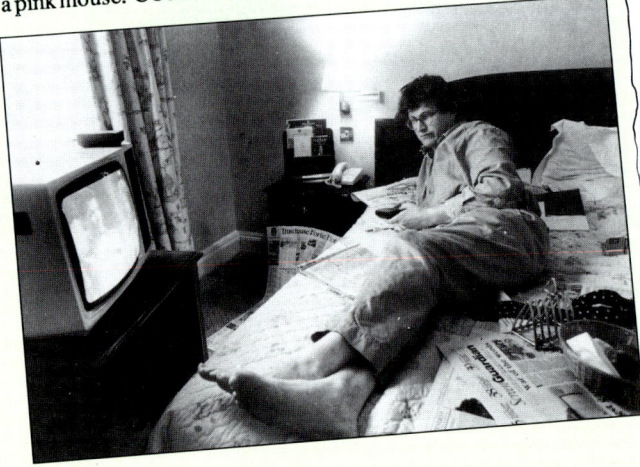

1 What do you think Alan Rusbridger learned from his 24-hour satellite TV viewing about:
   a the different kinds of programme available?
   b the similarities between countries and channels?
   c whether TV is mainly for entertainment or education?

2 What confused him about:
   a adverts?
   b time of events?
   c location of events?
   d language and accents?

3 'The world has become one big neighbourhood.' Has it?

4 Drawing the detail from your own TV viewing, and following a similar approach to the one in this article, write a free verse poem, or a commentary, or a note-book extract, entitled, *Zap!*

Research

1 Write a report on current developments in cable and satellite TV, setting out:
   a their advantages and disadvantages and the differences between them;
   b the ways in which they have changed and will change our lives;
   c how they will affect government control over TV in terms of censorship and regulations.

2 Look carefully at a magazine giving cable/satellite TV programmes and compile your own ideal viewing for a week of around two to three hours per day. Then compare your schedule with a partner's and note down the differences, with explanations, deciding on any changes you would make to your own list.

TELEVISION AND RADIO

Interviewing an Interviewer

Anita Bhalla is a Radio W.M. (West Midlands) reporter and a TV presenter. The *Radio Times* writes of her work as follows:

■ *East in West*, Radio WM's programme which serves the Asian community, begins a new series called 'Healthline'. The first of the initial six Healthlines deals with accidents in the home - how to avoid them, but what to do in the event of one happening. Later topics will be German measles, immunization, diet in pregnancy, weaning and looking after your heart. On hand to answer calls will be speakers of Punjabi, Hindi, Urdu, Gujarati and Bengali to act as interpreters when necessary. Co-presenter Anita Bhalla says, "Although East in West is of special interest to Asians, our programme is for everyone and I think English listeners will get a lot out of it."

Here are extracts from an interview with Anita Bhalla (A.B.) by Richard Mills (R.M.)

1 Read the transcript as if it was part of a play and talk about what you learn from it that you didn't know before.

A.B. From starting at W.M. I got offered a job to go and present Channel Four's first Asian programme on television . . . It was too late to train. And it was done for live which meant beforehand you had to sit down and talk to the researcher about the story-line. We had to know about the star, about his history, background, likes, dislikes, moods . . .

R.M. How do you find out somebody's moods? (*Laughs*)

A.B. (*Laughs*) Well, part of it's picked up but part of it is also a meeting before the interview. For example, when I was interviewing Gary Sobers and the whole team, he was coaching the Sri Lankan team, the evening before we met some of them, had chats with them, got a feeling of what they are all about. And they also get a chance to get to know you. Just to make it much easier the next day when you actually go and do the interview.

R.M. And then, in the studio itself, you have to get used to autocues and various signals.

A.B. Autocue is basically, if you're doing a piece to camera, erm, it is written up for you (**R.M.** Right.) and you read it out. Now, your interviews you can't obviously have written up. You have to think those through and memorise them yourself. And often you would write your own script because it's easier to say your own words than to say somebody else's words.

R.M. And then you also look for signals from various people in the studio?

A.B. Yes. There's usually a floor manager who will give you a sign to take it away. There's also a signal if your interview's only supposed to be three minutes and fifty seconds. Then, when you get to three minutes, you're given a signal. Fifty seconds. Ten seconds. Wind down and, you know, the cut also. So you have to, all the time, when the camera's not on you, be aware that there's a clock ticking by and you've got to work to that clock.

R.M. So you're answering so many demands, aren't you? You're listening to what the person is saying and trying to respond to that. You're aware of all the signals that are coming at you from people in the studio. (**A.B.** That's right). You're aware of the seconds ticking away.

A.B. And the camera. If you want to glance down at a paper or at the floor manager, you've got to do it when the red light isn't on your camera. (*Laughs*)

A.B. Now, I've just recently been doing some reports for Midlands Today television news and I've suddenly discovered I actually enjoy being the reporter. You get a chance to develop your story, to meet people, to direct the way the shots are going, what you want said, your own script, your own shots. Your own sort of story-line. And the entire piece is your own.

R.M. So you're responsible for that piece of news?

A.B. Yes. And that means you find the cameramen. You book the cameramen. You get your story-line accepted by the news editor. You go out and film your story and all kinds of horrific things can happen. You write your own scripts, so you have to book yourself a studio.

R.M. I'm amazed that you have to do all that yourself. I'd assumed somehow there was somebody else who organised it all for you.

A.B. No. You do all your form filling and booking and your own script. So television isn't all glamour. (*Laughs*)

R.M. No. No. What's the most interesting part of the job and what's the most boring part?

A.B. I think the most interesting part of the job is actually talking to people. The frustrating and the boring part is the sheer hard work that goes on before you get your programme presented on radio. The hard work is finding your interviews, finding your stories, the headaches of phoning people, arranging times, going out as a reporter if you need to, coming back, chopping it, putting it all together. That can be exhausting.

R.M. And that, of course, is what the viewer or the listener never sees or hears. They don't know all the work that's gone on.

A.B. No. That's the headache of the producer.

R.M. What's the most amusing thing that's happened? (*Laughs*)

A.B. Well, lots have happened. (*Laughs*) There have been incidents when one of us leaves the mike on when you've put a record on and you think nobody's listening and you start saying, 'Oh, I must go to the loo. I've been dying to go for the last ten minutes.' (*Laughs*)

R.M. And it's being broadcast to thousands of listeners?

A.B. Yes. (*Laughs*)

2   Copy this chart of Do's and Don't's for TV presenters and list as many further points as you can:

Do's	Don't's
1 Write your own script.	1 Don't work from someone else's script if you can avoid it.
2	2
3	3

3   Anita mentions 'horrific things' that can go wrong with a TV reporter's plans. What could some of these things be?

4   The role of the questioner (R.M.) includes:
   a   asking a question to stimulate further comment;
   b   summarising points made;
   c   commenting in a personal way;
   d   responding to a point made by A.B.;
   e   reinforcing an earlier point;
   Go through each of R.M.'s comments and label them a to e.

5   List three other questions you would like to ask Anita about her work. Then guess at what the answers might be.

Research

1   Carry out an interview, as if for radio.
   a   First, think of an interesting local person or topic and make arrangements for the interview.
   b   Then, think of three or four different aspects of the topic, working out particular questions you could ask.
   c   Practise the interview on your own or with a partner, using a tape recorder.
   d   Conduct the main interview, trying to make your questions sound natural and trying to enter into the discussion.
   When it's all finished, select the best bits to play back to your group when you tell them about the work you have done and what you have discovered.

2   Tape-record or video three or four radio and television interviewers and prepare a report for your group, with examples, on the differences between the interviewers, in terms of:
   a   how they treat their interviewee; (for example, Are they really interested/ mocking/aggressive/friendly?)
   b   the kinds of people and topics they cover;
   c   whether they or their interviewees are the stars;
   d   their humour;
   e   their interest and appeal to you, as a listener or viewer.

TELEVISION AND RADIO

Radio Plays

Your task in this Unit is to take an extract from a novel or short story which you have read and to dramatise it for radio.

Before you begin you will need to think carefully about what makes a radio play. To help you, here is a transcript of the introduction to Radio 4's eight-part serialisation of *Bleak House* by Charles Dickens. In it the first chapter of the novel is condensed into a sequence lasting just two minutes.

Read it carefully to give you some ideas about setting out your own work. It is set out as recommended by the Radio Drama Department of the BBC.

Some points to notice

a Names of characters are clearly separated from their own speech. They are in capital letters here, but they could be underlined or written in a different colour. They are in a separate column.

b Names are given in full throughout.

c Descriptions of sound effects or other technical direction are clearly differentiated from the parts intended to be spoken.

d Pages of script are numbered, and in rehearsal scripts each speech is numbered, starting afresh at the top of each page.

'BLEAK HOUSE' P.1

(FADE UP EXTERIOR SOUND. DISTANT. A CHURCH BELL TOLLS. SOUND OF A HORSE APPROACHING, TROTTING OVER COBBLED STREETS. SOUND OF RAIN FALLING STEADILY, SLOWLY FADING THROUGHOUT FIRST SPEECH.)

1. NARRATOR   London. Michaelmas Term lately over, and the Lord Chancellor sitting in Lincoln's Inn Hall. Implacable November weather. As much mud in the streets as if the waters had but newly retired from the face of the earth and it would not be wonderful to meet a Megalosaurus waddling up Holborn Hill. Smoke pouring down from chimney-pots making a soft black drizzle, with flakes of soot in it as big as full-grown snowflakes gone into mourning, one might imagine, for the death of the sun. Fog. Everywhere. Fog up the river among green meadows. Fog down the river among lines of shipping. Fog on the Essex marshes. Fog on the Kentish heights. And hard by Temple Bar, in Lincoln's Inn Hall, at the very heart of the fog, sits the Lord Chancellor, in his High Court of Chancery.
   (INTERIOR. NOISE OF VOICES, DISTANT.)

2. MR TANGLE   (Distant) .. and therefore, m'lud,

3. CHANCELLOR (Close) Mr Tangle?

4. MR TANGLE   (Distant) M'lud?

"BLEAK HOUSE' P 2

1. CHANCELLOR Have you nearly concluded your argument?

2. MR TANGLE   M'lud. No. There are variety points - feel it m'duty t'admit - your ludship.

3. CHANCELLOR Then we will proceed with the hearing on Wednesday fortnight. In reference to the young girl...

4. MR TANGLE   Begging your ludship's pardon - boy.

5. CHANCELLOR In reference to the young girl and boy, wards of the court now in my private rooms, I will see them and satisfy myself as to the expediency of making the order for their residing with their cousin. I will resume the matter tomorrow morning when I take my seat.
   (A GAVEL IS HAMMERED DOWN LOUDLY.)

6. SUITOR   (Screaming) My lord! Please ...
   (GENERAL UPROAR IN THE COURTROOM. SHOUTS OF 'SILENCE')

7. NARRATOR   The despairing voice is hushed and the ruined suitor hustled away, for the Lord Chancellor has vanished and everyone else vanishes too. The empty court is locked up. If all the misery it has caused could be locked up with it, and the whole burnt away in a great funeral pyre - why so much the better for other parties than the parties in Jarndyce and Jarndyce!
   (THEME MUSIC.)

If you can get a copy of *Bleak House* you may wish to read the opening chapter to compare it with this dramatised version. Would you rather read the book or listen to the play? Why?

Choosing your own book

Your choice of book will depend on your own interests, and what you have read, but bear these points in mind:

a Always have a copy of the book available for you to work from.
b Be familiar with the whole story before you begin.
c Don't be too ambitious. Choose a short extract and read it thoroughly.
d Choose an incident which is complete in itself.
e Choose an incident with a fairly small number of characters.

Constructing your play

Finally, these points are also based on advice given by the BBC Radio Drama Department to people wishing to submit plays to the BBC.

a A sequence in a radio play is not like a scene in the theatre or in a film. It may be several pages long – or just one line. But remember, of all the media, radio can most easily create boredom, and is very easy to switch off.
b When nearing the end of a sequence it is important to prepare the listeners, as subtly as possible, for the next one. They have no programme, and they can't see.
c Don't give lengthy stage directions for the producer's benefit. If the information is important it should be in the dialogue.
d Remember that the listeners will supply their own mental pictures to fit what they hear. Give them enough information to help them to do this, but not so much as to restrict or confuse them.
e When deciding on the number of characters in a scene remember that the only way a listener will know they are present is for them to speak or to be spoken to by name. If there are too many the listeners will become confused or will lose track.
f Sound effects are an essential element and need to be considered as carefully as the spoken words as the play is being constructed.
g Since radio involves only one of the senses it is important to provide a variety of sound which will hold the listeners' attention.
h There is no formula for writing a successful radio play. The best way to get an idea of what works and what doesn't is to listen as often as possible to radio plays.

Research

1 Tape-record a radio play. Listen to it as a class or in a small group and discuss the ways in which it follows the advice offered by the BBC Drama Department.
Transcribe two minutes of it, setting it out as *Bleak House* has been set out here.

2 Use a copy of *Radio Times* to find out what drama is produced on radio in any one week. Copy and complete this chart to show the following information for each play:

Radio Station (1, 2, 3, 4, other)	
Weekday & Time	
Duration (i.e. time taken)	
Series Title	
Play Title	
Author	
Producer	
Other comments	

What conclusions can you draw from your chart about radio drama?

TELEVISION AND RADIO

Take a letter

The *Radio Times* and *TV Times* always contain letters from listeners and viewers about radio and television programmes. These letters are written in order to:

- congratulate (for example, praising a programme)
- complain (for example, saying what you don't like about a programme)
- correct (for example, putting the producer right on a small detail)
- comment (for example, giving your views on a subject)
- question (for example, asking for information about one of the stars)

1 Which of these categories do the following letters fit into?

2 Discuss each of the letters and the issues they raise, saying whether or not you agree with the writer and why.

3 Discuss each letter title, saying what you think of it and why.

4 Write a reply to one of the letter writers, as if from the programme producer.

Good taste

A short while ago I noticed a tea-set in the Barlow household in *Coronation Street*, and last week I saw it again, but on this occasion Mavis Riley was using it. Are the props department on an economy drive or is it just a popular design?
Mrs Jane M Williams
Brecon
Powys

Carry the card

I watched with interest *The Gift of Life* (10 January BBC1). It was an excellent programme which fully portrayed the benefits of transplant surgery. I myself carry a donor card and I feel it's a pity that we can't adopt the American policy of asking relatives if loved ones could be considered as suitable donors . . .

I also feel that donor cards should be made more readily available and that we need more publicity to show the advantages of transplant operations . . .
(Miss) Susan Croft
Halesowen
West Midlands

Frog faux pas

What a pity Les Dawson chose such an unfunny subject as frogs' legs being chopped off to amuse the Queen at the recent Royal Variety Performance on ITV. Frogs' legs are obtained by hacking the legs from the living frog and flinging the rest of the body on a heap to die anything up to an hour later. The British do not eat frogs by tradition and should not encourage this cruel practice.
Mrs Jill Fowler
(animal artist)
Tring
Hertfordshire

Tragic error

I wonder what irresponsible person had that gormless Charlie Mycroft saying: 'Oh, you can't die from taking pills, you are sick first.' I wonder if some stupid person said the same to my daughter three years ago, when she took some headache pills to frighten her boyfriend and, despite being sick first, died horribly two days later. Perhaps writers should research their facts a bit more. We were told by the doctor at the time that 12 headache tablets taken at once and left in the bloodstream longer than six hours are lethal.
Hilda Grey
Llanelli
Dyfed

Be warned

I would like to express appreciation for the warning given on ITV before the film *Ordinary People*. I was looking forward to seeing the film, but on hearing that it included strong language I was glad of the opportunity to avoid it. I wish a similar warning could be put before all such programmes.
Mrs E Oldridge
Barton-upon-Humber

Going too far?

A workmate told me that a recent *World in Action* programme (ITV) showed film of an actual murder being committed in Japan. I am appalled that a broadcasting company should do anything so irresponsible. The television company that produced the programme, and the network that screened it, both share the guilt of being party to a detestable arrangement – accepting an invitation from murderers to take pictures of a man being stabbed to death. I don't know whether to be angry or to cry. Doesn't anyone in broadcasting see what the acceptance of this sort of thing is doing to this nation?
Mr Roy Gill
Fleet, Hampshire

No hope without soap

I'm addicted to the American soaps. I've been banned from watching them for a month and every time my favourite programmes are on and I'm missing them I feel like crying. I once had a crush on Joan Collins because of her role as Alexis. Is this normal? What can I do to prevent myself becoming a hard soapaholic?
Aileen Connell
Dumfries

Fruit-machine addiction

At last the media are recognising that fruit-machine addiction is as bad as a drug. We watched *40 Minutes: Jackpot* (21 January BBC2) and empathised with both addicts and parents.

Our son lost friends, employment, self-respect and almost his life trying to kick this habit. He too suffered night sweats and DTs among other withdrawal symptoms. Fortunately he was made of sterner stuff than we credited him with. His self-disgust and our continued support helped him rebuild his life, but only after we'd all been through a living hell.

We applaud the families who were brave enough to face the cameras . . .
(Mrs) Elizabeth Williams
Swansea
West Glamorgan

A real tonic

Thank you TV-am for the series on alternative medicine. There is a growing need for more programmes of this type. I work at a cancer centre in Aylesbury and alternative medicine is a lifeline for many patients. I was annoyed, however, at the flippancy of the presenter who could have put some people off. But Matthew Manning, the healer, was very interesting.
E Elliott
Buckingham

More music, less chat

I must put pen to paper to compliment Radio 1 for their experiment on Monday 18 January when we had the treat of more music and less DJ chatter.

I kept the radio on all day as opposed to normal when after about an hour I've had more than enough of the senseless drivel . . . I hope Radio 1 repeat this idea more often – preferably every day!
Martin Jackson
Droitwich
Worcestershire

What's afoot?

While watching American football on C4, I have noticed that some players have dark patches on their faces. Can you tell me why?
Mrs P K Ellis
Christchurch
Dorset

Research

1. Collect more examples of letters, either from magazines or from TV and radio itself and decide which of the five categories each letter fits into.

2. Write a letter to a radio or TV producer, or to the *Radio Times* or *TV Times*, about a programme or topic you feel strongly about. Report back to your group about your letter and the reply you receive.

TELEVISION AND RADIO

Eye Witnesses

Newspapers, radio and television depend on eye witness accounts of incidents.

Here are four such accounts, all taken from radio.

1. Practise reading the extracts out loud in your small group to capture the mood of each one. Discuss how the reading could be improved.

2. How can we tell that each extract has been spoken, not written?

3. Try to work out in each case:
   a. exactly what the description is about;
   b. what you learn about the speaker (age? sex? job? point of view?);
   c. who the audience is.

4. Work out two or three questions to ask each of the speakers, for information they don't give you in the extract.

5. Which extract:
   a. would have been said slowest/quickest?
   b. has the shortest sentences? Why?
   c. is the most dramatic? Why?
   d. is the most interesting? Why?

6. Choose one account and re-write it as if spoken by someone with a different point of view of the experience, for example, one of the boxers in A or a rescuer in D.

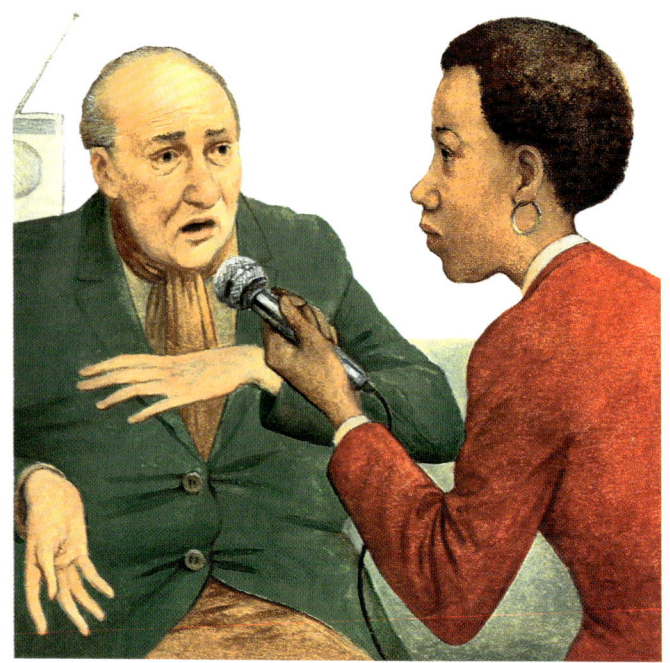

A Round nine and Marciano coming out to try and finish him now and he swings that right hand and that left and he catches Cockell straight away high up and Cockell fights back all right, just swinging away but not the same power. Marciano driving in on a tremendous right hand. Cockell's in trouble. Cockell is down from that right hand. Cockell is down. He is up at seven. He is up at seven. And the referee wipes his gloves and Marciano comes in for the kill. Lefts and rights by Marciano. A right across and Cockell throws again, again he swings and misses and almost goes off balance and Cockell is still there and Marciano not even pretending to box, swinging out with lefts and rights. And he catches Cockell on the back of the head. Cockell's down, down from a fall as much as from a punch and he is up again. I can't hear the count. About four.

B I could see the smoke billowing out behind me. About six people stumbled out afterwards and then, then, no-one, erm. We could hear some more people coming up behind and were shouting and erm people that who were on the street level were shouting encouragement, 'Come on, you're almost out, you're almost out.' But nobody else actually came out. Erm, some firemen threw some ropes down, to see if anyone was who would catch hold of the ropes but no-one did.

C As a Jew living in England I was much more terrified of the invasion than most English people were. I mean the English would have been inconvenienced, but the Jews would have presumably been exterminated. So we were extremely frightened of that. When the war started I'd been in England for about just over a year. I'd come as a Jewish refugee and had taken an au pair job, and got married just shortly before the war to an English undergraduate. The day war broke out we moved into our first house in Bury in Lancashire, and then a few months later when the invasion scare started and all Germans, whether they were Jewish or not, were interned, my father, who had come over to England just before the war, was interned. By one of those strange coincidences he was in the internment camp in Bury in Lancashire, the town where I lived, and as soon as my husband and I heard this we went a few miles outside Bury to this camp, and as it happened just when we arrived all the prisoners, or the internees, were having their exercise and were walking behind barbed wire, and I discovered my father looking rather dejected, and suddenly he saw me and of course, you know, looked very pleased. And he came to the barbed wire and I went to the barbed wire and talked to him. Then a Special Constable came up to my husband, who was wearing his Cambridge college blazer, and said, 'You know it's forbidden to talk to the prisoners,' and my husband said, 'My wife is talking to her father who is interned,' and so the Special Constable turned his back to the barbed wire, looked my husband straight in the eye and said, 'I'll be on again tomorrow from twelve till one, and the next day from five to six,' – or whatever it was – never actually saying, 'Come when I'm on,' but implying it. And so every day for a week we came to the camp when this Special Constable was on duty. He chatted to my husband with his back to me and my father who could converse through the barbed wire.

D

SURVIVOR: I woke up and heard a funny noise and wondered what it was. I got out of bed and when I looked outside I was in a sea. Well, I jumped out quickly and got a few clothes on and came in the sitting-room and of course the water was coming up and up and up, and I jumped on the bed settee first, and the water got up to my chest, and I thought I have got to get up on something higher than this. Well, this table was floating round the room and I got hold of the thing and pulled it along to the fireplace and, er, threw myself across it and of course the water was washing over me then, so I got on my feet and stood up and, er, there I stood until late Sunday.

INTERVIEWER: You stood on the table?

SURVIVOR: I stood on the table top until, pressed against the mantelpiece, until late Sunday; I should imagine it must have been about four or five o'clock. I was so exhausted by standing, I tried to get down on the table to sit but I lost my balance and me feet and legs went in the water and the water then was coming right up. I sat like that until I was rescued on Tuesday.

INTERVIEWER: On Tuesday?

SURVIVOR: On Tuesday about four o'clock.

INTERVIEWER: But you must have been there for three days.

SURVIVOR: Yes, I was there for three days.

INTERVIEWER: But did you have anything to eat?

SURVIVOR: No, I couldn't get anything. I was in the water and couldn't get at anything.

INTERVIEWER: Nothing to drink?

SURVIVOR: No, nothing at all. It was drink I wanted. But, er, the milk was on the table. I thought if only I could get that but I couldn't, and I had a nice little bottle of whisky my daughter brought me home from Ireland.

INTERVIEWER: Where was that?

SURVIVOR: That was in the dressing-table drawer in the bedroom.

INTERVIEWER: That is the place to keep it.

SURVIVOR: Yes well, I couldn't get it so I had nothing at all until they rescued me and took me to hospital.

INTERVIEWER: You were conscious the whole time, you remember?

SURVIVOR: Well, no, I kept losing myself but I knew I'd got to keep me senses, otherwise I should have gone into the water. I fought against sleep and I fought against unconsciousness.

Research

1 Tape-record from radio, or video-tape from TV, any ten minutes of a programme in which people are interviewed. Then study your material to work out the differences between interviewers and interviewees, in terms of:
   a who asks the questions
   b who talks more
   c who seems to be the expert
   d who (on TV) we see more of
   e who has a particular point of view to put across
   f who is in control of the discussion
   g who seems to 'win' the argument
   h who brings the discussion to a close
   From what you discover, draw up six points of advice for new interviewers.

2 Interview and tape-record someone at home, school or college, describing a dramatic/frightening/funny incident in their lives. Then transcribe two to three minutes of your recording by writing out the actual words spoken and including your own ways of indicating:

   • pauses   • volume   • intonation

   Use your material as the basis for a story or newspaper article or radio/TV report.

3 Arrange for three or four of your friends to witness the same brief event, for example, science experiment, home economics demonstration, piece of live drama, or video extract, and tape-record their accounts of what happened. Work as a group with the speakers to study the differences in the accounts. What do you learn from this about eye-witness descriptions?

NEWSPAPERS

Underground Fire

We are all strongly moved by the personal tragedies of other people which we see on television or read about in the papers. These tragedies might affect only one person or they might affect thousands. This Unit traces the coverage of a very serious event and shows how it was treated and reported in different papers and different media.

For discussion

1. How do you explain the different casualty figures in the headlines?
2. Which of the ten headlines are statements of fact? Which headlines use the most dramatic words?
3. Should such a story be the front-page lead item? Why? Why not?
4. There are differences in the papers between pictures, headlines, space and number of words given to the story. What are some of the reasons to explain the different treatment and coverage?

Newspaper	Headline	Lead story	Total no. of words	No. of pictures	Total surface area of pictures	Other comments
The Guardian	27 die in London Tube blaze	Yes	c 975	1	220cm	Story spread across top half of front page. Picture of police car and fire engines outside station.
The Telegraph	Thirty killed in King's Cross Tube inferno	No	c 660	0	-	Story in two large columns on right-hand side of front page. Paper lead story on U.S. arms report.
The Times	Nine die, 50 hurt as blaze hits Tube	No	c 255	0	-	Story in small left-hand column on front page. Paper lead story on U.S. arms deal.
The Independent	Four die in Tube station blaze	No	c 295	0	-	Story in large right-hand column on front page. Paper lead story on radiation danger.
The Sun	40 dead in Tube Inferno	Yes	c 275	0	-	Large headlines and story occupies two thirds of front page.
The Mirror	27 die in tube inferno	Yes	c 255	1	253cm	Large headlines, story, and picture of injured man occupies most of front page.
The Star	50 dead	Yes	c 475	2	402cm	Large headline, story, and pictures of entrance to underground station and one of wrapped up dead body occupies all of front page.
Today	Tube Hell	Yes	c 3,000	8 (including one in colour)	2433cm	Large headline, story, and colour picture of fireman being given oxygen occupies all front page.
The Express	Death blaze on the Tube	No	c 100	0	-	Story in small bottom left column on front page. Paper lead story on child abuse.
The Mail	30 killed in Tube Horror	Yes	c 460	1	240cm	Large headline, story, and picture of victim being comforted occupies all of front page.

Any major disaster story contains certain ingredients. These can include:
- a eyewitness accounts
- b expert opinion
- c brief summary of events
- d political comment
- e historical background
- f reaction from public figures
- g official statement

Read the following extracts from the coverage of a London Underground fire and label them **a** to **g**, as appropriate.

1
● At least 27 people died and hundreds were injured in a blaze 100ft below ground in a London Tube station last night.

2
It was quite clear that the smoke was getting quite thick by this time and that something quite serious was happening. So I stood in front of the escalator and tried to stop people by waving my arms and saying, 'Please don't go up the Up escalator, there's a fire starting.' But people just brushed straight past me and carried on walking upstairs.
Woman on radio

3

Page 244 NEWS

The Queen said she was deeply shocked to learn of the fire at King's Cross underground station.
She asked for her 'heartfelt sympathy' to be conveyed to the families of those died and praised the fire and police services for their courage.

4

I felt so helpless, I, I just couldn't, the the poor man was, like, you know, just standing there and collapsed and there was just smoke coming off him. It was ab, I, I just can't, unless you're there you you just can't, erm, do you know what I mean, you you just can't visualise. It was awful and there's nothing we could do. *(sigh)* I just hope to God those policemen who actually helped us got out themselves, 'cause they had no breathing apparatus at all and and they were young lads, you know, and they had no helmets. They were in disarray, I mean, they they were choking like everybody else, and, do you know, I mean, it, it, sorry, it upsets me a bit, but they were still standing there, helping people out, you know, even though they were choking themselves. Let's hope, God, it never happens again.

Man on radio

5

When you look at the amount of fire damage in a very large area, obviously there must have been a rapid spread of fire. One of the problems is, of course, with fires underground, especially when you've got concrete passageways and concrete tunnels, is that any fire within there, there is a tremendous build up of heat, heat which is retained inside the concrete. So, fire-fighting in those particular situations is extremely hazardous, extremely difficult.

Assistant Chief Fire Officer Radio

6

The death toll is the worst on the Underground since 43 people died at Moorgate on February 28, 1975, when a train ploughed into the end of the Northern Line branch tunnel.

7

Page 244   **NEWS**

Transport Secretary Mr Paul Channon has announced that there is to be a formal public enquiry headed by a senior QC into the King's Cross fire tragedy. Mr Channon told the Commons that 30 people died and 20 were injured in the fire on the underground yesterday. He expressed his deepest sympathy to the victims and their relatives and paid tribute to the rescue services. His sentiments were echoed from all sides of the House.

8

The more people going through, the more care should be taken to ensure that they are safe because even when it's lit and there's no smoke and no fire and no panic and no danger, you, you know and anyone who's been in King's Cross underground station knows, it's a, it's a veritable warren, a maze, even when you think you know your way.

MP for the area. Radio 1

1. What do you learn from each of these extracts that adds to your knowledge and understanding of the fire?

2. In what ways, (such as speaker/writer; audience; tone and effect), is:
   a   7 different from 4?
   b   6 different from 2?
   c   3 different from 8?

3. Which is the most interesting to you and why?

Research

1. *Either:*
   Over a period of a few days compare the treatment and coverage of a major story in two or more newspapers, on radio and television. Write a report on your findings.

   Or:
   Follow the day's reports of the same major event in several national newspapers and complete a copy of the table in this Unit to show the differences in coverage.

2. Take a radio or television news item and turn it into a brief report suitable for teletext. (Remember that teletext tries to inform viewers briefly of basic facts soon after events have occurred.)

NEWSPAPERS

Children at the Gate

This Unit shows how an event, the opening of a children's home, is presented to the press by the Government.

Children at the Gate is a play devised by a group of young people aged between 12 and 16 and scripted by a professional writer, David Calcutt. The play shows the experience of those involved. The press accounts give a very different picture.

In the opening scene a minister of a future government makes a statement to the press, in which she explains a scheme for setting up a number of Residential Homes to cater for children with special needs.

In between the minister's speeches are a number of one-sided 'conversations' which tell the audience something about the future residents of these homes.

SCENE 1

PRESS OFFICER AND MINISTER FACE THE AUDIENCE

PRESS OFFICER: Gentleman – and ladies – of the Press. With regard to the government's proposal for establishing a number of Special Residential Homes for disadvantaged young people, the Minister with responsibility for this scheme has prepared a statement for you. She will read this statement now, and will take no questions. Is that understood? Good. Minister.

MINISTER: Thank you. The aim of setting up these homes is to provide the special care, attention and education that is needed by children who have a physical, mental, or social handicap. Children who cannot really be catered for in the mainstream of the education and care system. As a responsible government, we feel a special responsibility to these children, and to see that they have the best chance possible of one day being re-integrated into society as normal and useful citizens.

(*Freeze*)

(*1ST PARENT enters*)

1ST PARENT: I've had enough of you. Understand? I've done my best, but my best isn't good enough, is it? I can't do any more. Shut up, and listen to me for once. You're always in trouble. Running away from school. Stealing. Fighting. I said shut up! Now it's the police. Where's it going to end, eh? Prison? You'd like that would you? What? Don't get clever with me. I'll wipe that stupid grin off your face in a minute! Anyway, I've decided. If I can't do you any good, perhaps they can do you some good in one of these new homes. Maybe they'll be able to knock a bit of sense into you there. Now, just watch it. Don't you dare use language like that in this house. No, you didn't learn it off me! You're going to get some discipline, you are. They'll teach you some discipline in there, and a few other things. I'm sorry. You're going and that's that! Sit down! I said sit down! Come back here! Now! If you don't come back here straight away. I'm warning you! I'm warning you, I said! Come back! I haven't finished talking to you yet!

(*Freeze*)

MINISTER: Among the many advantages of such a system is that we will be able to concentrate in these homes all the latest and most up-to-date equipment needed for the training and rehabilitation of these children. Equipment that normal schools and homes would never be able to afford. So, they will be more cost-effective. And the best teachers with special training will be in permanent residence so that they can build up a close relationship with the children over a sustained period of time. The family atmosphere that we hope these homes will engender will encourage the kind of caring attitude among the able-bodied children for their less able-bodied fellows that will be an integral part of their social education.

(*HEAD TEACHER enters*)

HEAD TEACHER: I'm afraid that this latest incident is the final straw. I cannot have my school constantly disrupted by the likes of you. And the disturbance you caused in the classroom this morning simply cannot be tolerated. Whatever your home or family problems might be, young lady, I have a school to run, and other children to think about. You have been given every chance and opportunity, and you've wasted them all. I'm afraid I cannot have you as a pupil at my school any longer. I've spoken to your mother, who I know is at the end of her tether with you, poor woman, and she has agreed with my proposal. The best course of action is to have you transferred to one of the new Residential Homes. I don't think you'll find much scope for causing disruption there. All right? Very well, then. Off you go.

(*Freeze*)

MINISTER: As for education, the emphasis will be on training. Training for the physically handicapped to help them overcome, or at least cope with, their disabilities, and training for the others to equip them with a useful skill or trade for adult life. The system will be rigid, but fair. Children, especially children such as these, do respond much better to a strict regime. It gives them the kind of security they need. And visiting by members of the family, certainly during the first six months, will not be . . . encouraged. We are of the opinion that the children will need a sustained period of time in which to settle down to their new environment without the upset that might be caused by such visits.

(*Freeze*)

(*2ND PARENT enters*)

2ND PARENT: It's for your own good, Beverly, you know that, don't you? They've got the best teachers there. Specialists. They'll be able to teach you to speak properly. I mean, you know I've tried my best, but it's got you nowhere. It isn't just your speech, is it? You're slow as well. I know you can't help it. It isn't your fault. They'll be able to deal with you properly in there. And I need a rest, Beverly. I do. It's worn me out, all these years. I can't help you any more. Now, don't try and say anything, Beverly. It's no good. I've made my mind up. What? What are you saying? I can't understand you. Stop it, Beverly. Shut up. You're getting yourself in a state. Stop it! I don't understand! That noise. It's just a noise. Stop it, shut up, I can't stand that wretched noise you make!

(*Freeze*)

MINISTER: In conclusion, let me say this. We know this is a radical proposal. But we have never shirked from radical and often difficult decisions. The times we live in – with increased disturbance and violence in society, especially among the young, with the resources of schools, the social services and the police being stretched to breaking point – in times like these, I say, radical proposals are needed, and they are needed urgently. I would hope that this scheme will not only be understood by the vast majority of the population, but will be welcomed with approval and praise.

(*Freeze*)

(*3RD PARENT enters*)

3RD PARENT: Don't take her! No. Leave her here! I can look after her! You've got no right! I never gave my permission. You can't do this! Leave her! Bring her back! Bring her back!

(*Freeze*)

1 In a group read the scene aloud in order to answer these questions:
   a What is the first clue that the government may not be as caring as it makes out?
   b How should the minister say her lines for them to be convincing?
   c Why is the direction *Freeze* given so often? What effect does it have?
   d What do you learn from this scene about each of the characters who are to be the residents of the new Homes?

2 Suppose you had been present as a news reporter when the press statement was made. Write a piece in support of the government's proposals, for either television or radio news or for a newspaper.

Scene 2, not given here, shows the children arriving at one of the Homes. Some are there because they have broken the law and are beyond the control of their parents and schools. Some are there because they have physical disabilities: one is blind; one is deaf; one refuses to speak; one is unable to walk. Scene 3 is a short one. The children enter, position themselves in a tight group and speak directly to the audience.

SCENE 3
(*Children enter and speak to the audience*)
STEPH: That was our first day at the home.
ALEX: The others didn't get any better.
DONNA: They treated us like slaves. Pushing us around. Giving us orders.
JULIE: And if we didn't obey them, we got what for.
REBECCA: We didn't dare put a step out of line.
LINDY: They were watching us all the time, just waiting to jump on our backs.
ASHLEY: They treated Spud like he's some kind of moron.
CHARLEY: All of us disabled kids – it was like they thought we weren't human.
JESSIE: Just something to be shut away and forgot about.
KELLY: There was nothing you could say, nothing you could do.
TARA: We were shut up in here, and nobody wanted to know.
LINDY: Every day was the same.
REBECCA: Get up at seven. Go to the showers.
JOHNNIE: Back to your room, get dressed, make your bed.
STEVE: Bed inspection. That bed's a mess! Make it again.
DONNA: Breakfast at half past seven, finished by eight.
TONI: If you miss it, bad luck.
STEVE: I had to make my bed again!
JOHNNIE: Shut up and get out!
STEPH: Back to your room, get your things ready for lessons.
JULIE: Lessons start at half past eight.
ALEX: And the day drags on. If you're lucky you get through it without being punished.
DONNA: We weren't lucky very often. There was always something.
REBECCA: Talking out of turn, making a mistake.
ASHLEY: Not paying attention. Wipe that grin off your face!
CHARLEY: They always found something to pick on you for.
JESSIE: Some way of humiliating us.
KELLY: Till we felt like giving up. But you couldn't give up. They'd get you for that as well.
DEBBIE: We just wanted to go home. But we couldn't go home. There wasn't any home for us any more.
JOHNNIE: Only this place, and every day the same.
STEVE: Grinding you down till you couldn't take much more.
TONI: Till you felt like you really were going crazy.
BEV: But we ain't crazy! There ain't nothing wrong with us, and we ain't crazy!
End of Scene 3

3 Read this scene aloud and answer the following questions:
  a Explain how this Scene is different in form from Scene 1.
  b Can you suggest a reason why it is written in this way?
  c What is the purpose of this Scene?
  d What do you learn about the way the place is being run?
    How does it differ from the promises made by the minister?

4 Suppose now you are a reporter who has been able to interview the children. Write a follow-up to your first piece giving the children's point of view.

NEWSPAPERS

Suspended for Stealing a Kiss

In this simulation several news teams gather information by interviewing people about a particular case and then, after discussion and planning, they write a news item for radio, television, or a newspaper.

There are five reporting teams and five people to be interviewed, so that five interviews may take place at the same time. One way of operating is to set a strict time limit for each interview, after which the reporting teams must move on to another person.

The case to be investigated

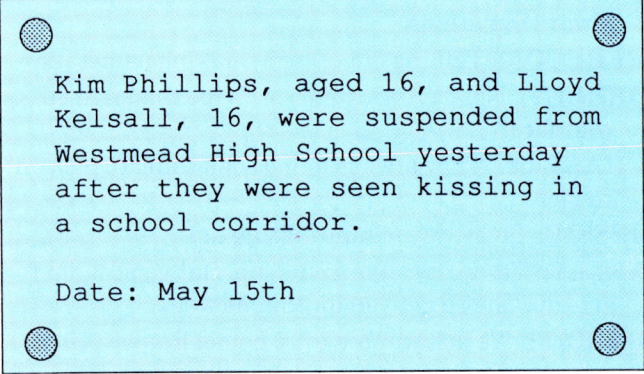

Kim Phillips, aged 16, and Lloyd Kelsall, 16, were suspended from Westmead High School yesterday after they were seen kissing in a school corridor.

Date: May 15th

Characters
Carole Phillips, Kim's mother
Jean Kelsall, Lloyd's mother
Robin Peters, schoolfriend of Kim and Lloyd
Helen Roberts, Head Teacher, Westmead High School
Graham Hulme, Fifth Form Tutor, Westmead High School

Interviewing teams
local television news
local evening paper
local weekly free paper
local radio news
national daily paper

Brief for interviewing teams

1. Decide on a name for your paper or programme. Decide also on different jobs within your team. It would be useful, for example, to appoint an editor, who will have the final decision on how the item is written.

2. Decide what sort of information you want. Plan a number of questions with which to begin your interviews.

3. Conduct your five interviews, taking notes on what the characters say, and, where possible, quotations which might be useful. (Do not try to catch out the role players with trick questions or with details of time and place. Try instead to discover their attitudes towards the case.)

4. When you have interviewed all five people decide what slant the story should have, its prominence and whether there will be a need for still photographs or film.

5. Draft your news item.

6. Agree as a team on your final version, editing and redrafting where necessary.

Brief for role players

1. Read through your role card carefully.

2. Decide on any additional information you think you may need to supply. Any details you invent should fit in with existing known facts.

3. Give an interview to each of the five reporting teams. Remember to stay in role at all times.

4. When you have given your interviews make notes on how you were treated by each of the five teams and on how you felt at being interviewed.

5. Use your notes to help you to write in role, as the character, *either* an entry in a personal diary or journal reflecting on your experiences of being interviewed; *or* a letter to a close friend telling of the experience.

6. Redraft and produce a final version of your diary entry or letter.

1. Record the finished radio and television bulletins on tape – or perform them live, or pass round your newspaper report.

2. Compare and discuss the treatment of the case by the different news teams under the headings:
   - Format
   - Content
   - Slant or Bias

3. Discuss the feelings and the treatment of the people who were interviewed. A possible starting-point would be for these people to read to the group their diary entries or letters. How does each person react to the final news items? What could they do about them?

Role cards

HELEN ROBERTS MA
You are Head of Westmead School and have done all you can to achieve high standards of discipline and academic work. Recently, at a school disco, you were distressed by pupils' behaviour which you thought too intimate for a public place. You had threatened to suspend Kim and Lloyd among others. You felt after this incident, in school time, you had no option but to carry out the threat. A few days off school would hardly affect their school work, but might shock them into a change of attitude.

JEAN KELSALL
You and your husband have been worried about Lloyd for some time. But you are very pleased now he has a sensible girl-friend. You like her and think she is a steadying influence on Lloyd. You know they are planning to become engaged. Lloyd has been offered a job in a butcher's shop where he works part-time now. You are worried about the suspension, but would rather not make a fuss in case it makes things worse. Lloyd won't talk to you about what happened. The letter he brought home said he was 'behaving in an improper manner'. You and your husband, and Lloyd, have to see the Head after half-term.

ROBIN PETERS
Kim and Lloyd are your friends, and you were with them when the incident took place. You'd all come back to school just after afternoon school started. Lloyd had left his bag in the CDT block, and it had gone. That meant he'd lost his History project too. Kim found the bag at last, stuffed behind a radiator. Lloyd kissed Kim on the cheek as they parted. You heard Mrs Roberts yelling as you hurried upstairs. You and Lloyd have both been in trouble at school recently.

GRAHAM HULME
You have been Lloyd and Kim's Form Tutor since they came to the school. You know other staff are worried about Kim's work, but you are well pleased with Lloyd's recent attitude. Since the promise of a job, he seems to have become more mature and responsible. You don't want to be disloyal to the Head, whom you respect, but you feel she may have over-reacted, and that suspension may be counter-productive. Teachers will be giving out holiday revision work which the two will miss. Kim said to you, privately, 'There's no way I'm staying on in the Sixth Form now.'

CAROLE PHILLIPS
Since your husband left six years ago it's been a struggle to bring up Kim. Now you're not too happy about her relationship with Lloyd. You want her to take A levels and go on to university. You fear suspension will spoil her chances. You think the Head is being ridiculous. Kim told you that after lunch she and Lloyd were going to different classes and he gave her a 'friendly peck on the cheek' as they parted. The Head rushed them to her office, went on at them at length and sent them home with letters to their parents. Your letter asked you to see the Head, with Kim, after half-term.

NEWSPAPERS

Photo and Be Damned?

Band Aid captured the imagination of millions of television viewers in raising money for starving people in Ethiopia. Here the chief organiser, Bob Geldof, writes about his argument with photographers. Should they take any pictures they like?

'You really do have to understand this. I do not want any pictures taken of me with starving children. We've seen them before, visiting politicians looking fat and concerned as they hold a child in their arms who is near to the point of death from malnutrition, who may well die the day after the western celebrities and their photographers have left the camp.'

'Christ, Bob, you know that's the picture we've been sent to get, you with one of the children who Band Aid is trying to help. That *is* the picture,' said Kenny Lennox of the *Daily Star*.

'I know it is. And it is the picture that I don't want. Can't you see how cheap it is. It's disgustingly sensational. It degrades the people involved. It's exploiting their misery to give you a nice shot.'

'But it's not like that. You're not here for publicity, we know that. You're here because you are trying to help. All we are doing is recording the horror which is the reality of the situation.'

'That's not how it will appear to people at home. It will simply be construed as shameful, distasteful and patronizing. You can take pictures of me in the camp. You can take pictures of the kids. But not the two together.'

I did not trust them. Earlier Kenny had told me that he was one of the photographers who had taken photographs of Princess Diana in her bikini when she was pregnant. In all other respects he was a nice bloke. He tried to keep certain problems off my back and you notice things like that. He spoke of his own child in relation to some of the kids we saw in a way that was sensitive and moving. But it was weird, as soon as he started to do his job he seemed to throw all sense of personal morality on one side. He told me how he had lain out in a boat for a couple of nights to get that bikini picture. He was clearly proud of himself.

'The public have the right to know,' he parroted.

'Right to know what?' I asked. 'Why do you want to hurt people? Did you take pictures of your own wife when she was pregnant and show everyone in the neighbourhood? Is the woman not allowed to enjoy her pregnancy in private? I don't suppose she went to the beach in her bikini again after that!'

In trying to defend himself he revealed that he had been one of the photographers who had prevented Elizabeth Taylor from going to mourn alone at Richard Burton's grave. Sometimes, he said, one photographer would be prepared to make concessions but was unable to do so because a competitor would refuse to do the same. She had risen before dawn to be at the grave before anybody else was up. When Liz got to the cemetery gates she had been confronted by photographers and had pleaded with them to leave her alone, just that once.

'We said we were all going to leave, and then one guy said he wouldn't go. What could we do? We couldn't leave him to be the only one who got the picture. What would our editors say?'

'So what happened?'

'Well, as it happened there weren't any pictures, because when we wouldn't go she didn't go in. She just went away.'

'So she didn't get the chance to say her last goodbye. Are you proud of that?'

'No, but if I'd gone the other bloke would have taken the picture anyway. So it would have happened whatever I did.'

'So because this woman is a star she has no right to mourn privately? Is that it, Kenny? That's unacceptable. By involving yourself with that you are just adding to that horrible cheapness and nastiness. You're a nice bloke, Kenny, but spare me your self justification.'

I went to each photographer and made each swear on his honour not to do it. When people actually do that, it becomes serious. They all did, even Kenny.

1 Whose side are you on, Kenny's or Bob's? Why?

Oxfam have faced this kind of problem for a long time. Here is an extract from an Oxfam newsletter.

Foreign news journalists line up their cameras in front of a starving child. Top news awards have gone to photographers who took pictures like these.
Picture: Wendy Wallace

'Drama' means vivid pictures. These moved us to act, but how do reporters get them? Nick Carter of the Guardian reported on how foreign journalists were working in refugee camps in Sudan:

"At $150 a night, the Khartoum Hilton is already crowded with television teams. The freelance photographers are the worst. We had one who spent three hours crouched by an old woman so that he could get a picture of her death."

Famine

A child
Much too weak to eat
Much too weak to move
Dragged from the crowd
From his starving family.

He sits there
All alone
Scared and helpless
On the hot sandy ground.

Two cameramen
Photograph his puzzled and bewildered look.
He turns his head away
Helpless and scared.

Is this what they mean
When they say
Other countries gather round
To help?
Is it really like that?

Zoe Guest

2 Read Zoe's poem, then write a piece of free verse to show the struggle in the mind of a photographer facing a starving child.

3 TV and newspaper editors are constantly making decisions about what pictures to show and not to show. Put yourself in their shoes and consider the arguments for and against publishing pictures of the following real incidents:
   a An Arab man jumps to his death from a crane in Regent's Park, London, at a public demonstration of 50,000 Muslims.
   b An unknown old lady commits suicide by leaping off the top of Beachy Head cliffs.
   c A soldier shoots a prisoner of war in the street.
   d A little boy is in tears beside the body of his mother killed in a street riot.
   e A man suspected of rape and murder is led by police into court.
   f Rescue workers try desperately to find earthquake survivors.

Research

1 Make a collection from newspapers and magazines of photographs which some people might complain about on the grounds of their:
   a lack of decency;
   b being too horrific;
   c not respecting privacy or grief.
   Label each of your photos **a, b,** or **c** and use the pictures to make out a case either for or against censorship.

2 Dramatic photos in newspapers and magazines seem to involve *either*:
   a personal tragedy, *or*
   b conflict, *or*
   c suffering, *or*
   d historic events.
   Make a small scrapbook of interesting and dramatic pictures. Write a brief statement by the side of each one, saying what it is about, and what you think of it, and labelling it **a** to **d**.

NEWSPAPERS

Silkwood

This is the story of Karen Silkwood who worked at a nuclear power plant. She died in a car crash in 1974, aged 28. Details of her work and her mysterious death were widely reported.

Here are four pieces about Karen from:
- a newspaper article
- a book jacket
- a radio report
- a novelisation (that is, a story based on real events)

They are all versions of similar events, but each is written in a different way.
- one is a powerful advertising summary.
- one is in spoken language, emphasising the mystery of what happened.
- one is a dramatic re-construction.
- one is a factual account, with short bursts of information.

1 First match these four descriptions to the four extracts, and say which is the shortest extract and why.

2 Choose one extract and say how it achieves its effect. Concentrate on:
   a how the writer talks to the reader;
   b the ways in which the writer attracts the reader's attention;
   c the pictures which come into your mind as you read.

Newspaper

Contaminate attempt on 'sleuth' alleged

OKLAHOMA CITY (AAP-Reuter). — A union official testified yesterday he was convinced someone might try to contaminate Karen Silkwood with radioactive material while she tried to gather proof of safety violation at Kerr-McGee's plutonium plant.

He said she was 'sleuthing' for the union.

Steve Wodka, of the Oil Chemical and Atomic Workers' Union, said he worked with Miss Silkwood on union problems at the plant in 1974.

He was testifying in a $11,500,000 negligence suit filed by Miss Silkwood's family against Kerr-McGee.

The suit claims that she was contaminated with plutonium a week before her death in a car crash on November 13, 1974. She allegedly was heading for a meeting with Mr Wodka and a reporter with proof of safety and records violations at the plant when she died.

Convinced

Mr Wodka testified that he was convinced Miss Silkwood was being watched while she was gathering information for the union, but he did not detail his reasons for believing that someone might try to harm her. The Union official earlier testified that he hoped to use Miss Silkwood's evidence to gain an advantage for the union in election and contract negotiations.

Miss Silkwood was discovered to be contaminated with plutonium on November 5-7, 1974, and her flat was found contaminated on November 7. Kerr-McGee has claimed she might have contaminated herself to dramatise the allegations against the firm.

Her family's lawyers claim that the company is responsible for allowing plutonium to escape its plant near Crescent, Oklahoma.

THE STORY OF KAREN SILKWOOD IS THE STORY OF THE FIRST NUCLEAR MARTYR.

More terrifying than THE CHINA SYNDROME - because it's true - the story of the death of Karen Silkwood is a shattering account of corruption, cover-up and death at the white-hot core of the world's deadliest and most powerful industry.

Karen Silkwood worked at the Kerr-McGee plutonium plant. When she became convinced that the company was taking horrific risks with radioactive material she decided to talk. But Karen Silkwood never made it to her meeting with the *New York Times*: she died when her car plunged off the road on the way to the crucial rendezvous, her body contaminated with radiation from an unknown source.

Was it an accident or was she murdered? If it was murder, who killed her?

The Killing of Karen Silkwood is the definitive account of the case which put the nuclear industry on trial.

Radio Report, 1979

Last year a protester painted the tantalising question, Who killed Karen Silkwood? on a railroad car for all to see. Tantalising, because very few people even knew who Karen Silkwood was let alone who killed her. She worked in fact as a lab technician for a corporation in Oklahoma City which produced nuclear fuel rods for nuclear reactors. She was a slim, fiery woman of twenty-eight and she'd harangue union meetings about how the company's working conditions were deteriorating. She was on her way to 'spill the beans', so she said, to a newspaper reporter – *The New York Times* as it happened – when she was found dead in her crumpled car beside the freeway.

Well, investigative reporters immediately moved in along with the union and her fellow protesters and came up with enough bizarre circumstances to fill a mystery novel.

She'd spoken of documentary evidence, of incompetent and even deceitful management, of x-ray pictures of fuel rods touched up to disguise evidence of dangerously faulty seals, of company inventories showing that as much as forty pounds of plutonium was missing and of medical records to show that she herself was so contaminated by plutonium that she was dying.

Company officials were suspiciously quick to arrive at the scene of the accident. The police dispatched one tow truck to the wreckage but recalled it. When the car *was* finally moved there wasn't a single paper in it or on the body and there were marks on the bumper that looked as if the car might have been forced off the road.

The autopsy revealed that Silkwood's lungs *did* contain a big overdose of plutonium. It was then learned that only nine days before she died she had complained to the Company that she was contaminated and they had searched her apartment and had discovered fragments of plutonium in her bathroom, her kitchen, and even buried in a cheese sandwich in her refrigerator.

Novelisation

NOVEMBER 5, 1974. It was Tuesday, eight days before the scheduled appointment with David Burnham. The afternoon sky was shadily aglimmer. Thin argentine clouds scudded towards the horizon. Karen passed through the security airlock shortly after one o'clock. She stored a baloney sandwich in her locker and went to the Met Lab. For two hours she sat at a desk and filled out specimen reports. Three o'clock: time for a coffee break. She monitored herself the way the rules said, using a portable alpha counter. The counter had a dial marked with radiation measurements, but otherwise it resembled a hot-air styler, and seemed as innocent. She held the counter inches from her hands, face, clothes. Its silence pronounced her clean. Returning, Karen taped on gloves and worked with a lathe in Gloveboxes Three and Six. At the five-thirty break, the alpha counter again made no sound. Karen went to her locker and ate a sandwich, then resumed work in the glovebox.

Six-thirty: this was her real supper hour, but she had plans to spend it in the file rooms. *Rrrrit. Rrrrrit.* The sound was a diamond-back's warning. 'I'm hot! My hands are hot!' Karen's shout carried into an adjacent lab. An HP heard and came running. He took her to a darkroom and enlisted a woman clerk, who helped peel the layers of cotton and plastic off Karen. Polythene fingertips dropped everything into a bag for burial. A new smock got Karen down the hall to the first-aid station, a room small and white. Off came the smock, and Karen went into a tall shower, the nozzle turned to full pressure. Water sluiced down her body. She dried off with towels and hair-dryer and retested herself; plutonium still lined her nasal passages. Dabbing with cotton swabs, flushing with a rubber-bulb irrigator, she finally showed clean.

3   Go through the first three extracts carefully (excluding the novelisation) and draw up two columns about the story, as follows:

	Facts	Theories
a	Karen was contaminated with radio-active material.	She deliberately contaminated herself.
b	Her dead body was found in her smashed car.	She was deliberately forced off the road.
c		
d		
e		

4   Write a short story based on Karen's last hours of life, between the time she leaves a café, carrying documents, to the moment when she is found dead in her car.

Research

1   Hire the video film *Silkwood* for your group. Discuss the way it presents Karen's story and the kind of person she was. Write about one especially striking scene in the film, showing how it takes Karen's side.

2   *Either:*
Write to two or three nuclear power plants around the country, asking for information about tourist visits. Then collect extracts from the leaflets you receive, and from newspapers and magazines, which show how the industry is being marketed and advertised. Present these in the form of a brief scrapbook with commentary.

Or:
Write to any conservation pressure group, such as Friends of the Earth, for information on their views and activities. Present extracts of the leaflets, with brief commentary, in your scrapbook.
Exchange your scrapbook with a partner and discuss the arguments for and against nuclear power.

MAGAZINES AND COMICS

Magazine Spotting

Magazines are written for particular groups of people (audiences) and in particular ways which editors feel suit those audiences.

1. Talk about the following extracts and say who they seem to be written for.

2. Try to match the extracts with these magazines:

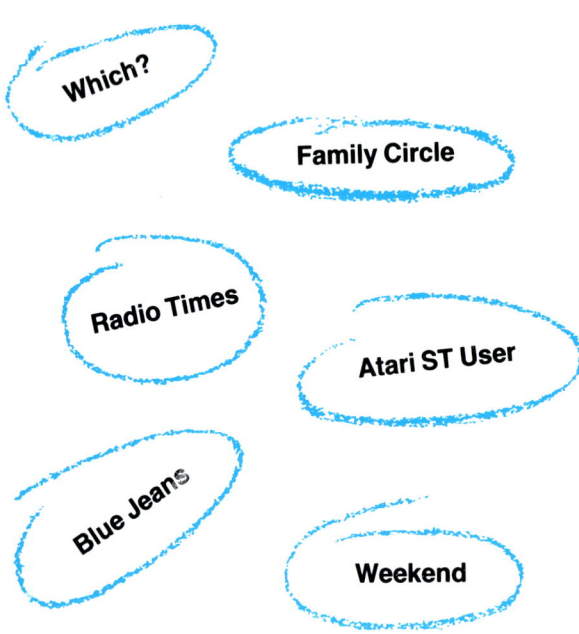

In each case give reasons for your choice.

A

The perfect answer to fruitful revision could be a quiet place where it's easy to concentrate. But that doesn't work for everyone. Some feel cut off and unable to concentrate if they're wholly banished, especially if used to working among classmates or family noise. So individuals have to find the place that suits them best.

- For those who want quiet, try the loft, spare room, garden shed (somewhere where they don't usually go might be less distracting for them.)
- Try the library's reading room, for quietness and company at the same time.
- A peaceful corner of your garden, or a friend's, could suit outdoor types.
- Revising in a public place helps some (we've heard of a girl who went round and round London's Circle line tube while cramming for her exams).
- Many schools send pupils home to revise - if that doesn't work, ask the head to put aside a revision room at school.
- Whichever place they choose (we've had reports of 'in the bath', 'on the loo', and 'in the cupboard under the stairs'), make sure it's warm and well-lit.
- At intervals, offer contact and comforts from the outside world, like tea/coffee and biscuits.

B

IN THE supermarket looking for a particular flavour of crisps for the kids, she has to ask a stranger to point them out to her.

At a bus stop, a bus arrives with its destination clearly shown, but she needs to enquire where it is going.

When she wants to send a note to the school, her 12-year-old daughter has to write it for her.

Her affliction? At 35, the mother of three young children, she cannot read or write.

C

'ME? Modelling in a fashion show?" I gasped. 'Oh Jill, that's great! Thank you for organising it!'

My best friend looked surprised. 'Eh? I didn't say you could be a model,' she said, looking embarrassed. 'I said I'd asked if you could help out. I meant as my dresser. There are going to be lots of quick changes.'

'Your dresser?' I was astounded. It was my turn to be embarrassed now. What a fool I'd made of myself, thinking Jill has fixed it up for me to model clothes too.

'Sorry if I raised your hopes,' she said. 'But there's no way you could model too - all the other girls are professionals. I was only asked because I'm the reigning Carnival Queen.'

'Yes, of course. I was being silly,' I muttered. 'OK, Jill. I'll be your dresser.'

I couldn't think of anything worse, but it'd look so obvious if I refused. I didn't want everyone to know how jealous I was of Jill.

D

In this report, we're concentrating on safety restraints for children. But there's a message here for car passengers of all ages: belting up matters - in the back as well as the front. It's tempting to imagine that you would be cushioned from the results of an accident just because you're not at the front. In fact, unbelted back seat passengers are at a risk to themselves and to their fellow travellers, especially in a head-on crash (the most common kind). In a 30mph crash, the risk of chest injury to a belted-in front seat occupant is nearly doubled when there's an adult loose in the back. You, the unbelted back seat passenger, could then hurtle on forward, piling into the dashboard and ending up in the front footwell or through the windscreen. You might think it would be possible to brace yourself against being thrown around. Think again: in the split second of a 30mph smash, your body might have to withstand forces of more than 20 times your own body weight. If you've been drawing comfort from the accident statistics that show only a fifth as many back seat passengers killed or injured as front seat victims, don't. Although you may be marginally less at risk in the back on certain kinds of crash, the main reason for the difference is simply that fewer people travel in the back of cars. Unfortunately, the drop in deaths and serious injuries for front seat occupants (130,000 fewer in the two years after seat beltwearing became compulsory than in the two years before) was not matched in the back: the number of serious injuries stayed the same, and the number of deaths rose.

E

AN ADVENTURER'S LIFE is a busy, but exiting, one. No sooner have you finished rescuing the kidnapped heir of Emperor of Ezzibonn, than along come the Guardians of The Golden Gizmo to ask if you can please pop over because they want to discuss your helping them recover said Gizmo which some light-fingered villain has half-inched with the intent of using it to take over the world.

To prove my point, Microprose has brought out Ultima IV for the ST, and it shouldn't be too long before Electronic Arts brings out an ST version of The Bard's Tale II. It obviously feels that an adventurer is never really content unless he's got plenty of new tasks, puzzles and dangers to face.

Ultima IV, subtitled Quest of the Avatar, is a massive graphics-orientated strategy adventure which offers a playing time of anything from 100 hours upwards. Your main objective is to transform yourself into a better person through courage, truth and love.

F

Ramsay Street is reaching fever pitch this week with Clive and Susan's wedding due to take place in a few days. At long last it looks as if domestic bliss is within the grasp of former deliverer of gorillagrams Clive (Geoff Paine, below). But we've all seen the strange way Susan behaves when the demonic Paul is around, and since that gripping episode with the runaway pram could Susan be having second thoughts about Clive as a babysitter for son Sam?

Research

1. Choose any magazine which interests you and do a survey to show its:
   - range of content (what is in it?)
   - apparent audience (who is it for?)
   - range of forms and writing styles. (See question 4.)

   Present your findings in the form of a report, either oral or written, to your group, using extracts from your chosen magazine to illustrate points you make.

2. Visit your local newsagent and, with permission, make notes on the range of specialist and general magazines, dividing them into categories or groups which you decide on.
   Interview the newsagent, if you can, and ask about:
   - magazine sales (who buys what?)
   - magazine stocks (how does the newsagent decide what to order?)
   - magazine distribution (where do copies come from and where do unsold copies go?)

3. Think about two of these magazines and list some other kinds of article you think the magazine might contain.

4. Think about the form in which each extract is written and try to match the following forms with the right extract, **A** to **F**.
   - review (of computer program)
   - review (of TV programme)
   - story
   - report
   - feature article
   - advice

5. Choose two of the extracts and write the next paragraph for each of them in the same style and the same form as the original.

6. Which extract interests you most and why?

MAGAZINES AND COMICS

Brief Encounters

How are quality magazine articles planned and put together? This Unit describes the process step-by-step.

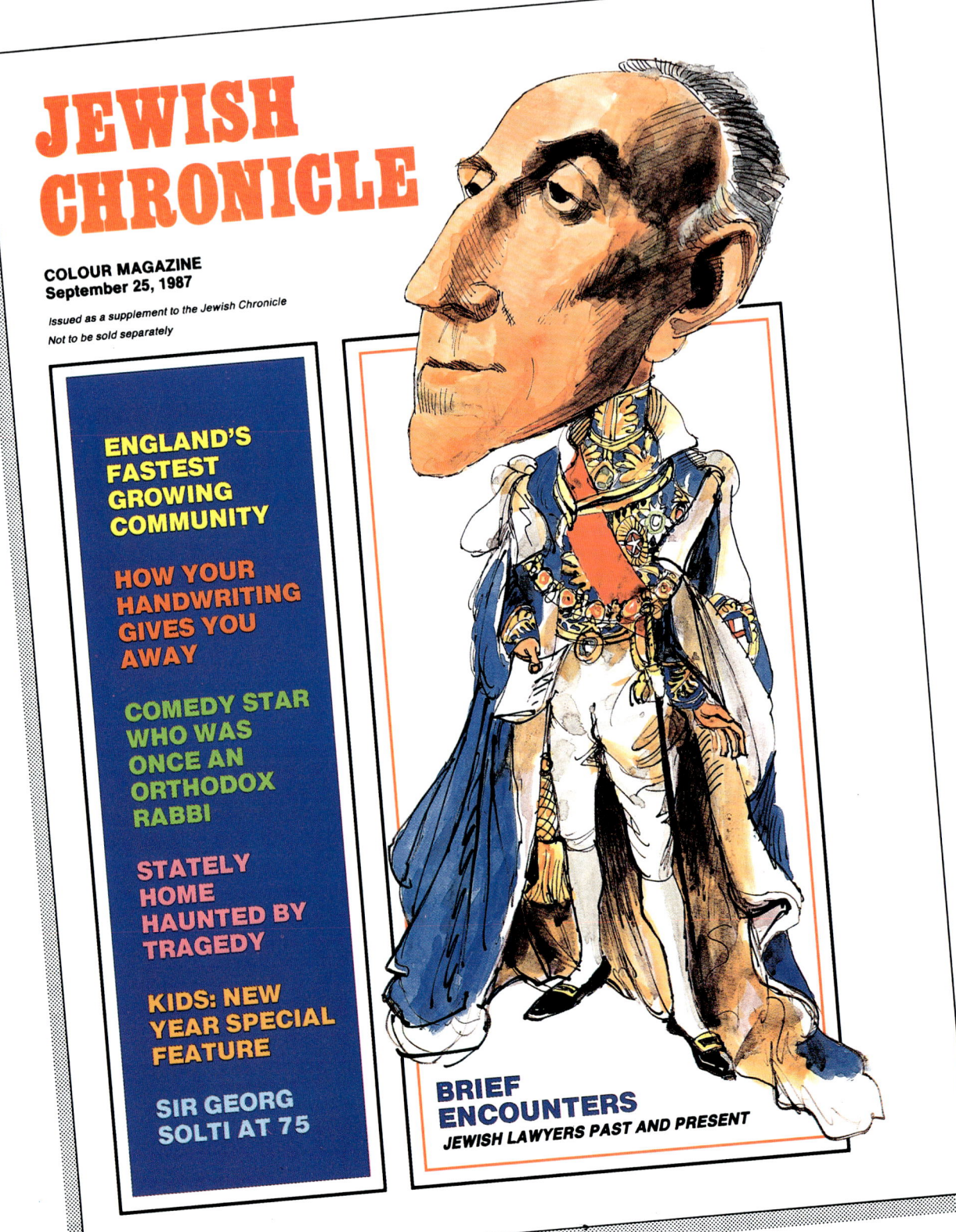

The *Jewish Chronicle* is widely regarded as the world's leading Jewish newspaper. Founded in 1841, it is published in London and is aimed mainly at the estimated 300,000 to 400,000 Jewish men, women and children living in the United Kingdom.

It is a weekly, appearing on the news-stands every Friday and covering a whole range of political, cultural, religious, leisure and domestic topics.

Four times a year the *Jewish Chronicle* publishes a colour magazine, which is issued free with the newspaper.

The following pictures will give you an idea of how a colour magazine article is put together. This one arose out of a discussion between the editor, Gerald Jacobs, and freelance journalist, Carole Field.

Since a number of Jews have had very distinguished careers as lawyers and made useful contributions to English Law over the years, Carole wondered whether the subject of Jews in the Law would be a suitable one for a colour feature.

1 Carole, whose husband is a barrister, makes the point that law is still a popular career choice for many young Jewish men and women.

Gerald and Carole compile a list of names of lawyers based both on their general knowledge and on Carole's research into the subject. Some of these are historical figures and some are prominent lawyers practising today.

It is decided that the article will be based on interviews, historical research and some general comments about Jewish lawyers and their work. Gerald gives Carole a *deadline* (a date by which the article must be completed) and a *length* (the approximate number of words he wants her to write).

These enable him to draw up a *schedule*, which is a list of articles for the magazine showing how many pages each one will take up and specifying when each part of the process needs to be finished to comply with the printer's own deadline.

2 Gerald decides that Carole's article should be illustrated by photographs and by cartoons in colour.

He gets in touch with illustrator Charles Front and suggests to him the names of four lawyers (three living and one dead) as possible subjects for cartoons. They discuss the style in which the cartoons might look best. Charles draws a few rough sketches to demonstrate his ideas.

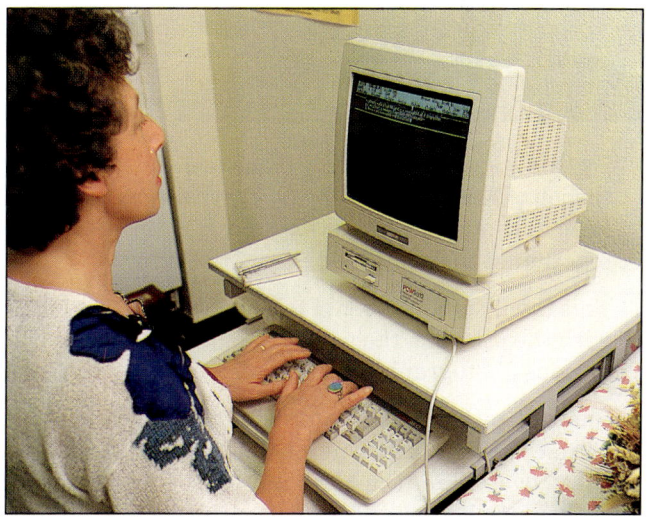

3 Having completed her research and interviews, Carole sets about the task of whittling down her notes into one clear and interesting article. Often the hardest part is deciding which bits of information to leave out!

4 Charles is mainly having to use photographs and sketches in history books as a basis for his drawings. But he is also going to spend some time in the High Court in London observing judges and barristers, to help him get the details right, including the correct colours and styles of robes and wigs. To ensure accuracy, he checks the window of a well-known legal outfitters.

5 By this stage, various threads have developed. It is the job of Kate Pentol, Gerald Jacobs' secretary, to keep hold of them all, making sure they come together at the right time.

This involves a number of telephone conversations with the printers, the writer, the illustrator and various photographic agencies.

She will gather photographs of people referred to in Carole's article from a number of sources, including the *Jewish Chronicle*'s own reference library. The magazine's editor, and art editor, Lee O'Herlihy, will make a selection from these for publication.

6 When the article is finished it is sent to the *Jewish Chronicle* offices where Gerald Jacobs will read it through, making any cuts, corrections or alterations he considers necessary. This procedure is called *sub-editing*, or 'subbing'.

Once the editor is satisfied, Carole's 'subbed' original is sent to the printers, sometimes by special messenger, and sometimes, as here, by means of a facsimile machine. This transmits a copy of the original document to the printers using the telephone lines between the two offices.

7 Once the printed article (set out in strips of paper, each of which is known as a *galley proof*) is ready and Gerald has decided on a title for it, and all the photographs and cartoon illustrations are available, the pages are planned and designed in the art department.

Here Lee, the art editor, is in consultation with Gerald and Charles about the possibility of using one of the lawyer cartoons on the magazine's front cover.

8 The final product – not only inside the magazine but on the magazine's cover. Here are some of the cartoons which accompany the article.

The cover cartoon, along with brief summaries known as *cover lines*, is intended to tempt readers to pick up the magazine, look into it and, everyone hopes, enjoy it.

Rose Heilbron

Louis Jacques Blom-Cooper

Arnold Abraham Goodman

1. Several people are mentioned in the commentary. Jot down brief notes about the jobs done by: Carole Field; Charles Front; Kate Pentol; Lee O'Herlihy; Gerald Jacobs, saying:
   a. who is employed full-time by the *Jewish Chronicle* and who is freelance?
   b. who is mainly concerned with words and who with pictures?
   c. who has the greatest responsibility and why?
   d. whose job most appeals to you?

2. Think of a short phrase to describe each of the nine stages. The first two could be:
   1. Approach to the topic
   2. Discussion with the cartoonist.

3. Look carefully at the photographs illustrating each of the nine stages and say what they tell you about:
   a. the people doing the jobs;
   b. the conditions they work in;
   c. the different ways in which they get their information.

4. What have you learned, which has surprised you:
   a. about the process involved in writing a magazine article;
   b. about the *Jewish Chronicle*?

5. Why are cartoons used?
   Is it to:
   a. attract the reader?
   b. provide an interesting contrast to a black and white photo?
   c. add humour?
   d. make fun of the law or of Jewish people?
   e. make a boring subject interesting?
   f. give a job to a cartoonist?
   g. show the character and personality of the people portrayed?
   Which cartoon do you like best, and why?

6. Quiz your partner on the meaning of the technical terms used in this Unit:

weekly	illustrator
news-stand	cartoon
colour magazine	reference library
article	sub-editing/subbing
editor	freelance
deadline	original
length	facsimile machine
schedule	galley proof
publication	

Research

1. Working in a group of four or five, as here, write an article, with illustrations, on any subject which interests you and which would be suitable for a particular specialist magazine. (Look carefully first at the magazine you have in mind, to get to know its style and presentation.) Your completed article could then be sent to the editor for possible publication.

2. Choose any illustrated article from a specialist magazine. Which stages in the writing and development of the article can you identify? Which stages do you have to miss out and why?

3. Prepare a brief report for your group about a specialist magazine or newspaper which is written by and for members of an ethnic minority group. Give details about:
   a. what is in it (its contents);
   b. how it is written (its style);
   c. how it appears to the reader (its presentation).
   Finally, describe your own reactions to the publication.

MAGAZINES AND COMICS

Record Reviews

Pop music is a major part of the media industry. Many new records are released every week. One way in which we find out about the latest releases is through record reviews.

These extracts from one person's review of six pop singles are taken from a pop magazine. Important details, such as the titles and names of the groups or singers, have been deliberately omitted. Read through all the reviews before attempting the tasks which follow.

This is the person who used to be the most swooned-upon American sibling the world has ever seen... and now he's back. Which is a pity because he's no longer the very essence of innocent boyhood charm, but a man. And thus he's grown up and gone all serious on us, creating a song that's a monstrous drip of a thing about leaving his heart on a sand-dune which doesn't sound at all healthy. What a shame.

...contains the wheezy grizzlings of a magical singer... grazing over a winking piano, some very grand 'n' gospelly backing singers, a large orchestral thronging and sensible non-drippified lyrics about that most perplexing of human 'emotions' – staring goofy-eyed at a silent telephone.... If this isn't a hit I'm going to kill myself. Well I'll be slightly annoyed at least.

So often they thump out the same old synthesized ploddings but this one's definitely more memorable because it's... well it's creepy.

They're Britain's Brightest Pop Group and this is their greatest blustering pop wheezle... it's about something... significant (though I haven't quite worked out what yet) and it sounds exactly like something else (though I haven't quite worked out what yet). This single proves once and for all that they have wit, intelligence, brevity, humour and the sparkliest, nippy pop tunes ever created.

❑ There's far too much keyboard plinking in the guise of 'soul' music dribbling round the planet these days... but at least these plinkings aren't flimsy... it's a proper pop song; bumping all over the place with trumpeting brass bits and swaying violins.

...this is a moodler – all lilting twangy noises, fluffy organy bits and some guffings about 'feeling the tears'. Quite nice if you're in the mood for being pathetic.

1 Discuss these reviews in a small group. Here are some starting points:
   a Together compile a list of the unusual expressions or invented words the reviewer has used. What do they mean? Why have they been chosen?
   b Do you find any parts of the reviews amusing? Which? Can you explain why?
   c How would you describe the tone of these reviews? (sarcastic? humorous? serious? rude? offensive?) What makes you think this?
   d What can you work out about the reviewer's own tastes in music?
   e What kind of audience is the reviewer writing for?

2 a On your own choose the records you think are the reviewer's best two and worst two.
   b Discuss your choices with other members of your group and try to arrive at a group choice.

3 Write your own reviews of three current chart singles, without mentioning titles or performers, and see whether someone else can identify them.

Newspaper reviews

Here are some extracts from newspaper reviews of a Michael Jackson concert.

1. Which of these three extracts is closest to how you feel about Michael Jackson? Why?
2. These three reviews concentrate on Michael Jackson's dancing, clothes, stage effects and video images. They say little about the music. How important to you is the music?
3. Describe the song and dance routines of any other pop star you have seen, either live or on video, as if to someone who had never seen the star. Say what he/she looks like, how he/she dresses, moves, sings and acts with the group and how the audience reacts.

MICHAEL JACKSON took Britain by storm last night as he wowed Wembley with a blistering performance that would put any pop star to shame.

Proving once and for all he is the greatest THRILLER of them all, Wacko Jacko gave his all.

In two hours of sheer magic, the Peter Pan of pop, played his heart out to 72,000 adoring fans.

He twirled, strutted and spun — knocking spots off his own dancing idol Fred Astaire.

He appeared on stage at 8.20 pm behind a puff of smoke as shots of his famous feet were beamed by the video cameras across the stadium.

The crowd went wild and Wacko went cracko opening the first of 14 British shows.

Michael hit the stage in a black and silver military-style suit.

But halfway through the first song, he had stripped off the jacket to reveal a silver lurex top.

Red torch flames shot from the stage and his public roared as he hopped, skipped and jumped from one incredible dance routine to another.

POP CONCERTS have not after all been superseded by video, they have just remodelled themselves on video principles instead.

The musical finale was a piece of pure circus in which Jackson disappeared into a silver shroud on a platform at one side of the stage, only to re-emerge moments later and in yet another costume — crouching on an hydraulic arm projected above the heads of the audience at the front.

Add to this a welter of wizz-bang fireworks, a white female glam-rock guitarist sporting a colossal mane of peroxide hair and Michael himself — wearing a gorilla's head one moment, lit up like a Christmas tree the next — and you start to get the picture.

This is pop gone to Disneyland via Hollywood.

There isn't a lot in Jackson's music to phone home about. If you were to name your 10 favourite songs, I doubt there would be one of his among them. But he dances with a taut, stabbing precision which defies his compadres to miss a beat. He embodies perfection, and he makes it look painful.

He's a peerless showman even in a football stadium. Costume changes are manipulated with a magician's slickness, through the ghouls-and-zombies routine. The live show is like the videos, but more so, and for every dizzying spin and reverse-walk he pulls off in the flesh, the dazzling video image alongside does it 10 times better.

Research

1. As a group project review the current top ten singles or LPs. Either mount your work as a wall display or produce a magazine. You could include photographs, biographies or other information about the artists and lyrics of the songs.

2. Describe the differences in the experience you have when you:
   a listen to a disc;
   b see a video of the same group;
   c attend a live performance of that group.
   Include in your account some cuttings from music magazines or newspapers to illustrate the points you make.

3. Select two or three very attractive record album covers and tell your group why you think they are so effective, bearing in mind such features as:
   - colour
   - wording
   - image
   - impact

MAGAZINES AND COMICS

Photo-story

Many teenage magazines contain photo-stories in which dialogue accompanies posed photographs. Here is some advice given by a major publisher of such magazines to people interested in writing for them.

Some hints on writing photo-stories

Photo-stories vary in length, but most are between 24 and 30 frames.

Setting out a script

There are no hard and fast rules about this, but it would be helpful if you could type your scripts in double spacing. (For various reasons, stories sometimes have to be changed and this allows room for the alterations.) Make sure that the photographer's instructions, dialogue and captions are set out regularly and clearly. You don't have to provide any photographs.

Remember that a script is told in a visual way. The storyline shouldn't be too complicated and should move smoothly from frame to frame. Captions can help a lot, but they should be used sparingly and mainly for the purpose of necessary explanation, where it is better to use a caption than a sequence of photographs. They are also useful to indicate changes of time and place, e.g. 'Later . . .' and 'That night at the disco . . .'

It's also the job of the writer to provide the photographer with a rough idea of the kind of photograph required for each frame. Try to visualise the story as it will appear, and remember that a lengthy sequence of similar photographs will tend to bore the reader.

Finally, don't spend too much time racking your brain for a title – we usually use our own anyway – but always include one for identification purposes, and remember to number pages and frames.

Characters

The most important aspect of a good story is that the characters come over through the dialogue, which should be crisp and lively. Always begin with a photograph and dialogue which will catch the readers' imagination and make them want to read on.

Character shows in what is said and how it's said. Try to give your characters individuality; people don't come off assembly lines and an unusual side to a heroine's character can bring her to life.

Avoid having characters telling each other things they already know, e.g. 'As you know, Alison . . .'

In emotional stories, the idea is to let the reader 'live' the story by identifying herself as the heroine. Let her take the emotion slowly. You should spend some time letting the heroine express her thoughts through dialogue. There is no strict rule, but the 'first person' approach is probably best for emotional stories.

Story Content

Most of the possible romantic themes have already been done, but they can be revived by putting them into a new setting, by lively dialogue or by an unexpected change of direction. This needs imagination.

Aim for an entertaining but simple style. Use language that the reader can identify with (within reason!).

'Flashbacks' can be used to build up character or cover a longer period of time, but overuse can be confusing and should be avoided.

Try not to go over the top with exotic locations and dozens of characters. The stories must be practical in terms of photography. We occasionally use 'ghost' stories, but remember that there is a limit to the special effects a photographer can produce.

Stories can be dramatic, sad, tense or amusing. Above all, though, they should have a romantic element involving the emotional problems of teenage girls.

Stories must reflect life today. We aren't looking for a meeting, a romance and a wedding all in the one story.

Here are eleven frames of a published photo-story called *Tales out of School*.

1. Using six headings taken from the publisher's advice, comment on how well or how badly this photo-story matches the required format. The headings are:
   - Dialogue
   - Identification
   - Location
   - Style and language
   - Practical photography
   - Modern life

2. The frames shown on page 61 are numbers 7–17. Describe the pictures and write the dialogue (or a summary of it) for each of frames 18–27. Try to follow the earlier advice, for example:

   Frame 18 Photo shows Jane walking to school the next day. She is day-dreaming about Mr Jarrett. Her diary is sticking out of her school bag.
   Frame 19 . . . .
   Frame 20 . . . .

   Now read a poem, *The Seduction*, which has some of the features of a teenage magazine story.

The Seduction

After the party, early Sunday morning,
He led her to the quiet bricks of Birkenhead docks.
Far past the silver stream of traffic through the city,
Far from the blind windows of the tower blocks.

He sat down in the darkness, leather jacket creaking madly.
He spat into the river, fumbled in a bag.
He handed her the vodka, and she knocked it back like water.
She giggled, drunk and nervous, and he muttered 'little slag'.

She had met him at the party, and he'd danced with her all night.
He'd told her about football; Sammy Lee and Ian Rush.
She had nodded, quite enchanted, and her eyes were wide and bright
As he enthused about the Milk Cup, and the next McGuigan fight.

As he brought her more drinks, so she fell in love
With his eyes as blue as iodine,
With the fingers that stroked her neck and her thighs
And the kisses that tasted of nicotine.

Then: 'I'll take you to the river where I spend the afternoons,

When I should be at school, or eating me dinner.
Where I go, by myself, with me dad's magazines
And a bag filled with shimmering, sweet paint thinner.'

So she followed him there, all high white shoes,
All wide blue eyes, and bottles of vodka.
And sat in the dark, her head rolling forward
Towards the frightening scum on the water.

And talked about school, in a disjointed way:
About O-levels she'd be sitting in June.
She chattered on, and stared at the water,
The Mersey, green as a septic wound.

Then, when he swiftly contrived to kiss her
His kiss was scented by Listerine
And she stifled a giggle, reminded of numerous
Stories from teenage magazines . . .

When she discovered she was three months gone
She sobbed in the cool, locked darkness of her room
And she ripped up all her *My Guy* and her *Jackie* photo-comics
Until they were just bright paper, like confetti, strewn.

On the carpet. And on that day, she broke the heels
Of her high white shoes (as she flung them at the wall).
And realised, for once, that she was truly truly frightened
But more than that, cheated by the promise of it all.

For where, now, was the summer of her sixteenth year;
Full of glitzy fashion features, and stories of romance?
Where a stranger could lead you to bright new worlds,
And how would you know, if you never took a chance?

Full of glossy horoscopes, and glamour with a stammer;
Full of fresh fruit diets – how did she feel betrayed?
Now, with a softly rounded belly, she was sickened every morning
By stupid stupid promises, only tacitly made.

Where were the glossy photographs of summer,
Day trips to Blackpool, jumping all the rides?
And where, now, were the pink smiling faces in the picture:
Three girls paddling in the grey and frothy tide?

So she cried that she had missed all the innocence around her
And all the parties where you meet the boy next door,
Where you walk hand in hand, in an acne'd wonderland,
With a glass of lager-shandy, on a carpeted floor.

But, then again, better to be smoking scented drugs
Or festering, invisibly, unemployed.
Better to destroy your life in modern, man-made ways
Than to fall into this despicable, feminine void.
Better to starve yourself, like a sick, precocious child
Than to walk through town with a belly huge and ripe.
And better, now, to turn away, move away, fade away,
Than to have the neighbours whisper that 'you always looked the type'.

Eileen McAuley

1. Compare the photo-story and poem in terms of:
   - plot
   - what each girl might have learned.

2. Each piece offers a picture of what boys and girls are like. Discuss the image of the boy and girl given in the photo-story and the poem.
   How might each account be different if written from the boy's point of view?

3. The photo story used the cliché, 'like a lost sheep', a phrase so overused it has lost its force. Pick out the clichés in the poem (such as his eyes as blue as . . .). How are they changed in the poem?

4. Use the main incidents in the poem to compose a photo-story.

Research

Do a survey of some teenage magazines and prepare a talk for your group to show:
Either:
- The image of boys and girls which the magazines promote.
Or:
- What things the magazines see as being important in life.

Magazines and Comics

Not So Comic

The strip cartoon comic format can be used for serious purposes. Here are two examples.

Part I

When the Wind Blows is the story of a gentle, simple, elderly couple who do their utmost to follow the official instructions to prepare for nuclear attack. The bomb is dropped and despite their efforts they find themselves dying a lingering death from radiation sickness.

The story now exists as a book, a stage play, a radio play and an animated film. Here is part of a page from the paperback book:

1. The author, Raymond Briggs, uses comic conventions (that is, special cartoon techniques) to tell the story. Discuss the effects of some of these conventions in this extract, including:
   a. the different kinds of speech bubbles;
   b. the different kinds of print;
   c. the ways in which the page is made visually interesting.

2. Briggs has been criticised for making Hilda and Jim too simple-minded. He replies: 'They were based on my parents really. Not so much my father, but my mum was very much one for not thinking and getting on with the dusting. Very obedient, law-abiding people.' Write what you can discover from this extract about the characters of Jim and Hilda. How do you feel about them?

3. Here are two different views of Briggs' work:
   'These are not books at all, merely strip cartoons.' (Headteacher)
   'This book should be compulsory reading for young and old alike.' (Newspaper)
   What are your views? Write a brief statement, using all the arguments you can think of, to persuade your readers that this book should, or should not, be in your school/college library.

Part II

This extract, from a cartoon Shakespeare series, is taken from the middle of the play *Macbeth*, where three assassins ambush Macbeth's enemy Banquo and his son Fleance. They manage to kill Banquo but Fleance escapes.

1. Many people find Shakespeare's language difficult. Which parts of this extract, if any, do you not understand? How does the strip cartoon format make it easier to follow?
2. Which is the best box, and why?
3. Why are the figures drawn with blank faces?
4. Look at the last scene. Why is it shown as it is?
5. Some people might argue that presenting Shakespeare in strip cartoon form is the wrong way to bring great works of literature into the classroom. What do you think?

Research

One illustrated Macbeth book took the artist a full year to complete. Look at the following sequence to see the stages it went through.

- Decide how many pages in final book.
- Research about the play and the costumes.
- Write out the words of the play.
- Cut up words on to double-page layout boards.
- Have rough drawings in pencil approved by publisher.
- Final drawings in pencil.
- Colour in pencil drawings.
- Do lettering.

1. Prepare a proposal for a publisher in which you make suggestions and give examples under some of these headings, for a serious strip cartoon book on a subject you care strongly about.
2. Find another example of a serious strip cartoon book and write a review of it, for your group, in terms of its: subject; language; visual presentation; comic conventions; impact and interest.

FILM

What's in a Film?

This Unit is about ways of promoting films by posters.

Richard Attenborough's *Cry Freedom*

In an interview, Robin Behling, Creative Director of the design company responsible for the poster for the film *Cry Freedom,* spoke about problems facing designers of film posters.

One problem was having to condense ninety minutes of drama and spectacle into a single image that people would remember. A special difficulty with *Cry Freedom* was that the film was a very serious one, dealing with the important issues of apartheid, Soweto and injustice.

Robin Behling said, 'We produced one version of the poster with black and white hands through chains. It was a very powerful image, but it overstressed the apartheid theme of the film.' This, he thought, would have put some people off. So, parts of seven pictures were put together to make the final poster, which is a single image, as shown here.

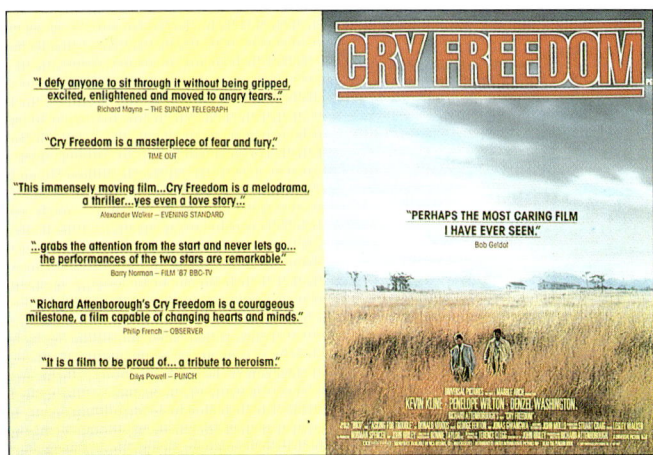

1 What is suggested by this poster?
2 Do you think that advertisers are right to play down important aspects of a film in order to make it a box-office success?

Examining the Posters

Look at the film posters which follow then choose one, other than *Jumpin' Jack Flash,* to examine in detail.

1 Look at the written information. For the film you have chosen make out a chart like the one below and fill in all the available information. Show, by putting a cross on the line in the right-hand column, the relative size of the lettering used on the poster for each piece of information.

What else could be said about the written information?

	Information	Size of lettering V. large — V. small
Title of film	Jumpin' Jack Flash	X (large)
Director	Not given	
Producer	Not given	
Female stars	Whoopi Goldberg	X (large)
Male stars	Not given	
Home video Distributor	CBS-FOX	X (small)
Release date	Not given	
Certificate	Not given	
Other written information	She's armed, She's dangerous. There's a British Agent trapped behind the Iron Curtain . . . The odds are against him . . . his only hope.	X (small)
	Boy! Is he desperate!	X (small)

2 Look at the visual information.
   a Describe in detail the picture used on the poster, either by writing it down or by talking to a partner.
   b What does the picture tell you about the type of film being advertised?
   c What part of the picture most stands out? How? Why?

3   Make a comparison.
When you have examined one poster in detail look again at all the others. Working in a small group discuss how each of the posters is meant to appeal.
Are they meant to attract your attention mainly to:
- the stars
- the director
- the type of film
- anything else?

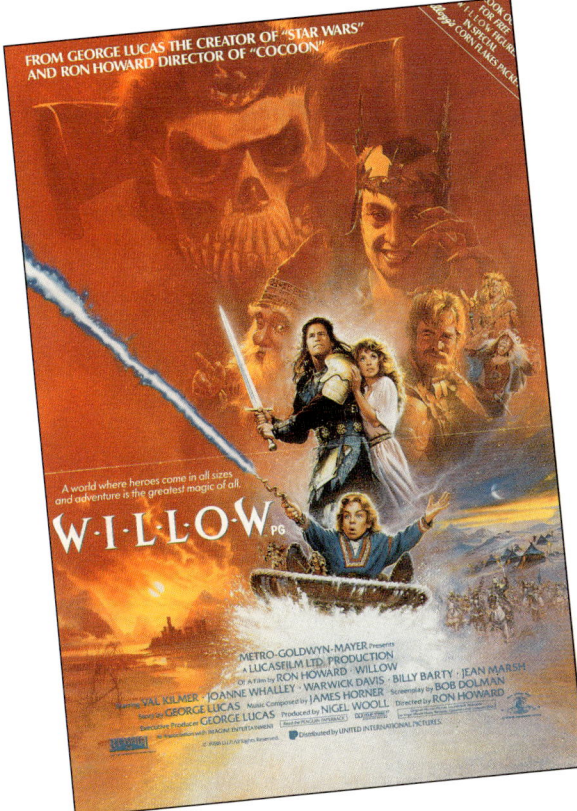

Research

1   For any film or video you have seen recently,
    Either
    Design an original poster, and then explain your design to a partner.

    Or
    Describe in writing what your poster would contain, explaining the thinking behind the design. Put yourself in the position of a design consultant having to explain the poster to the film-maker. Think about such features as:
    - image
    - appeal
    - target audience.

FILM

The Man From Snowy River

The Australian film *The Man From Snowy River* is based on a famous poem written in 1890 by A. B. ('Banjo') Paterson (who also wrote *Waltzing Matilda*). It is not unusual for novels to be made into films but very rare for a full-length film to come from a poem, especially when that poem is built around only one incident.

Briefly, the story in the thirteen verses of the poem is this: A valuable colt has escaped from a station (ranch) and joined the wild bush horses (brumbies). A group of crack riders gathers to recapture the colt. Among them are white-haired Harrison and Clancy, a drover (cowboy), both excellent riders. Harrison wants to leave behind an undersized lad from the Snowy River area, but Clancy supports the boy. The riders find the wild horses and follow them to the mountains. At this point the climax of the poem comes:

When they reached the mountain's summit, even
    Clancy took a pull –
It well might make the boldest hold their breath;
The wild hop scrub grew thickly, and the hidden
    ground was full
Of wombat holes, and any slip was death.
But the man from Snowy River let the pony have his
    head,
And swung his stock-whip round and gave a cheer,
And raced him down the mountain like a torrent down
    its bed,
While the others stood and watched in very fear.
He sent the flint-stones flying, but the pony kept his
    feet,
He cleared the fallen timber in his stride,
And the man from Snowy River never shifted in his
    seat –
It was grand to see that mountain horseman ride.
Through the stringy barks and saplings, on the rough
    and broken ground,
Down the hillside at a racing pace he went;
And he never drew the bridle till he landed safe and
    sound
    At the bottom of that terrible descent.

Of course, the un-named man from Snowy River brings in the wild horses and becomes a legend.

Obviously, the film-maker had many problems to solve in turning thirteen verses into an eighty-minute film. Here is an account of some of the decisions they made.

The names had to become characters, be given life and background, and other characters had to be woven into a story to bring them all to the brink of that wild ride.

The screenplay took a team of writers, much consultation, many drafts and three years to become a shooting script.

Along the way, the 'man' became young Jim Craig who came down from the mountains when his father, Henry, was killed in a logging incident. The white-haired, hard-riding Harrison is made a curt, tough American who came to Australia for gold and stayed to make his money from cattle and racehorses.

He has a pretty, independent-minded and spirited daughter, Jessica.

Paterson himself is brought into the story as a friend of Harrison. He arrives on the train with the thoroughbred colt from Old Regret.

Spur is another character. An eccentric goldminer who lives alone in a ramshackle mountain hut, he bears an uncanny resemblance to Harrison and seems to carry with him some mysterious secret of past bitterness.

Harrison's colt is both a star of the film, and a key element in the plot. Jim first meets the horse, and Jessica, when he steps in to calm it as it is being led off the train at the railway yards. Jim then seeks a job with Harrison.

Through it all run the 'wild bush horses' with the menacing stallion at their head. In the past his appearances have brought disaster and it is left to Jim to answer the challenge and end the tragedies.

Merrijig, 220 kilometres from Melbourne at the foot of the Great Dividing Range, was chosen as the film's location. Sets were carefully researched and constructed. Harrison's home-stead was built. Costumes and details such as farm machinery, carts and harnesses were given the same care as the film makers reconstructed the 1880s beneath the same mountains.

The 'cracks' who 'love hard riding' were found in the mountain men and their horses. They still ride with the same break-neck skill and daring that Paterson observed.

With Jim and Jessica, the story is given both romance and legend. Jim is the suitor prince who must test his courage and his manhood to win both the princess and the mountain kingdom. It is the heroic ride that finally achieves this and confers on the boy the title, the Man From Snowy River.

The producers needed a big-name actor with international appeal to ensure the film's commercial

success. The American actor, Kirk Douglas, was contracted for half-a-million dollars with the possibility of earning another half-million from a percentage of the film's gross takings. Douglas plays both Harrison and Spur.

In one scene the 62-year-old Douglas is required to ride out ahead of 40 thundering horsemen. In a close-up shot his face is to look grim and wild-eyed.

In filming the scene Douglas was commended on his acting. However, he said that knowing if he fell off at that speed, 40 thundering horsemen would ride over the top of him, appearing grim and wild-eyed wasn't really all that difficult.

A relatively unknown Australian actor, Tom Burlinson, was picked from 2000 auditioning actors for the part of Jim Craig and Sigrid Thornton was already selected for Jessica Harrison. Stalwart of Australian movies, Jack Thompson, is Clancy of the Overflow.

The horses were just as carefully selected and expertly coached. The 'colt' had to be every inch a thoroughbred, spirited and yet controllable. A long search finally singled out the racehorse, Aces Wild.

In seven months at Merrijig all those actors, extras, set designers, support people, photographers and horses turned Paterson's now extended ballad into a full-length feature film.

Scene 110 story board

Another stage in preparing a screen-play is story-boarding. Story-boards help to explain scenes in visual terms.

For the climactic scene in which Jim breaks alone from the horsemen and gallops over the ridge and down the mountain side, the director shoots equal to four times the length of the entire movie. This six hours had to be reduced by the film editor to 10 exciting minutes.

The storyboard extract makes it look simple. Illustrated are the first three of 12 frames that were meant to indicate how Scene 110 should be filmed. Notice the way the story is translated into pictures.

110 – 50 We are going to cover this shot with several cameras. Basically we are showing Jim on his horse straight over the top of us into virtually nowhere. An enormous leap that everyone else has been scared to make but Jim does it after shouting, cracking his stockwhip and off he goes.

110 – 51 Close up Clancy and Paterson. Clancy closes his eyes and turns away as a reaction to Jim's leap. We see Paterson virtually open-mouthed watching the ride. Continue this shot on for lots of reactions of Paterson and lots of reactions of Clancy to be used later.

110 – 52 A profile, Jim's horse landing and scrabbling away after he has just done the leap off the cliff.

Changes to the poem

1 What changes did the writers make in developing the film from the poem in terms of:
   - the characters?
   - the plot?

2 What other solutions were reached by the production team in:
   - choosing the actors?
   - choosing a location?
   - training horses?
   - helping the film to be a commercial success?

3 Writing a screen play means developing an idea into a film story. Often there are the following stages:
   - **Synopsis** a short outline of the story.
   - **Story-outline** the full plot of the film, written as a short story.
   - **Scene-outline** the story is broken down into numbered scenes. (There could be about 120 scenes in an 80-minute film.)
   - **Treatment** the scene outline is expanded in detail.

Using what you have learnt from the two verses of the poem and the article write a synopsis or a story-outline, of *The Man From Snowy River*.

4 The story-board on page 72 shows particular shots. Why has the director chosen these angles? What effects does he want to achieve?

5 Prepare story-board sketches plus description in up to five frames for the final scene where Jim brings the wild horses back.

Research

Choose a book or a story you know well and write either a synopsis or a story-outline of it. Say what particular problems you would expect to face and what changes you would need to make in turning the book into a film.

FILM

Hope and Glory

Where does the story of a film come from? Some come from novels, or incidents in the news, or historical events, or an odd idea. This Unit is about a film which grew from the childhood memories of its director, John Boorman.

He writes, 'The enterprise began with stories told to my children at bedtime. They seldom wearied of my adventures as a child during the war: air-raids, barrage balloons, shrapnel, doodlebugs, crystal sets. Chamberlain's speech announcing the onset of the Second World War is the beginning of the film. I remember every detail of that hour and have tried to render it in the scene.'

1. INT. ROHAN HOUSE: BACK GARDEN. SEPTEMBER 1939. DAY
Colour.

Raking down a line of suburban gardens lit by a late-summer sun. Heads move back and forth above the fences that divide the narrow strips of land, moving to the sound of unseen lawn mowers.

In one of these gardens are two children, BILL *(aged eight) and his sister* SUE *(aged six). They are sprawled out on the lawn, heads and hands intent on something hidden from view in the lush vegetation of a rockery garden. Beneath those flowers and plants is a dark mysterious forest, shaded by huge leaves, and broken up by towering boulders. Mounted figures of medieval knights ride in, guided by* BILL's *gigantic hand. A wizard appears in the path of the riders who draw up sharply.* BILL *gives an impression of neighing horses.* SUE's *face looms up between large leaves. She makes the sound of a spooky wind.*

2. INT. ROHAN HOUSE: DINING/LIVING ROOM. DAY
In the room, the mother, GRACE, *in droopy flowered frock, crosses, floats towards the walnut wireless and, with trembling hand, switches it on. Its green dial glows. She glides back and drapes herself behind an armchair in which her husband,* CLIVE, *sits solemn and motionless.*

3. EXT. ROHAN HOUSE: GARDEN. DAY
The sound of the lawn-mowers ceases abruptly. BILL *looks up sharply. The neighbours' heads come to rest on top of the garden fences. They turn, listening.* BILL *inclines his head towards the french windows, sensing the dread moment. He walks towards the door and is framed there. He regards his parents.*

4. INT. ROHAN HOUSE: DINING/LIVING ROOM. DAY
They look back with unseeing eyes. Young BILL *gathers fragments of the announcement.*
CHAMBERLAIN: (*Voice over*) . . . those assurances . . . by eleven o'clock . . . a state of war . . . that this country . . . at war with Germany. (*The boy catches his mother's eye. In the garden,* SUE *sings.*)
SUE: (*Singing, out of shot*) Flat foot floogie with a Floy Floy, Flat foot floogie with a Floy Floy. (BILL *turns to his sister.*)
BILL: Stop that, Sue! (CLIVE *is startled*) She just sings it. She doesn't even know what it means. (*An older sister,* DAWN, *fifteen, stumbles into the room in a nightdress.*)
DAWN: Where are my stockings? I can't find my stockings!
(*Her mother,* GRACE, *interrupts her with outstretched arms.*)
GRACE: Dawn, darling. They've started a war again. (GRACE *says it as though announcing that dinner is served, but her voice is torn by a sob as she holds* DAWN *in her arms.*) (*Whispering and sobbing*) We mustn't frighten the little ones.
(DAWN *is appalled by her mother's display of sentiment. She wrenches free.*)
DAWN: I don't care! I want my stockings!
(CLIVE *gets up, blazing. He seizes* DAWN *and shakes her.*)
CLIVE: Stockings? War! Don't you understand! War!
DAWN: I don't care!
CLIVE: War! War!
(GRACE *inserts herself between them.*)
GRACE: Clive. Don't. Dawn, please.

5. EXT. ROHAN HOUSE: GARDEN. DAY
BILL *calls out from the garden. He is jumping up and down, pointing at the sky.*
BILL: German planes! German planes!
(*They run out.* GRACE *sweeps little* SUE *into her arms, burying her face in her bosom and rushing back into the shelter of the house.* DAWN *and* CLIVE *scan the sky for planes. There are none.*)
I did see them. I did.
DAWN: He's the worst liar.
(DAWN *swings a fist at* BILL *and chases him into the room, raining savage blows upon him.*)

6. INT. ROHAN HOUSE: DINING/LIVING ROOM. DAY
Father is white with rage. He seizes them, one in each hand. Mother cowers with SUE.
BILL: I thought I saw them.
(*DAWN lunges at BILL. The GRANDMOTHER enters, tall, frail, elegant, deaf.*)
GRANDMA: Is it peace in our time?
GRACE: (*Shouting*) No, Mother! It's War! War!
GRANDMA: Or what?
GRACE: War! War! War!
(*The wireless begins to play 'God Save the King'. Father immediately lets go of the children and stands rigidly to attention. The others simmer down and shuffle into stiff and still poses. GRANDMOTHER, who perhaps cannot hear the Anthem, is baffled, shakes her head.*)

7. EXT. ROSEHILL AVENUE. DAY
The sirens sound the air-raid warning. They call out over the rows of semi-detached, lower-middle-class suburban houses. Some of the occupants burst out of their front doors, turning in frenzied circles, craning at the heavens.

8. INT. ROHAN HOUSE. DAY
The rigid family once more jerks into movement at the sound of the siren, looking fearfully out of the french windows, hiding under the table, clutching each other. The siren stops. They wait, anxiously. Silence. Even the birds stopped singing at the wailing of that first siren. This was perhaps the worst moment of the war, the first moment, when war was still an unknown dread thing. The siren again, but this time, a long sustained note.
CLIVE: That's the all-clear. Testing. They were just testing.

9. EXT. ROHAN HOUSE: GARDEN. DAY
CLIVE walks tentatively into the garden, looking up, shielding his eyes against the sun. The others join him, one by one.
GRACE: Such a beautiful day, too.
(*All search the clear blue sky. The sound of the lawn-mower starts up again where it left off before the war.*)
SUE: (*Singing*) Flat foot floogie with a Floy Floy.

As the opening of the film these scenes have to:
- introduce the main characters,
- set the scene and start the narrative, or story.

1 **The characters**
What do we learn from the script about Bill, Sue, Clive, Grace, Dawn? What sort of people are they? Say what you have discovered about the relationship between each of the parents and each of the children, and between the children themselves.

2 **The story**
There are many ways to start a story. One way is to begin with a settled world. This settled world is then broken up, disturbed or disrupted by some event. This is what happens in the opening scenes of *Hope and Glory*.
Copy out this chart and fill in the parts of the opening scenes which help to build up these two different feelings. The first part is done for you.

	Settled, normal life	Disruption
Sc 1	It is a sunny day in late summer. You can hear the sound of lawn-mowers.	Sue makes the sound of a spooky wind.
Sc 2	Clive and Grace are listening to the radio.	Grace's hands are trembling.
Sc 3		The lawn-mowers stop very suddenly. Bill notices and stands at the door.
Sc 4		

3 What is the point of opening the film with Bill and Sue playing with toy soldiers?

Stories in books are linked together by words, paragraphs, chapters. Films are linked by shots and scenes. As we have all seen many films, we are used to the way one scene is connected to another.

4 Look again at the script of the opening scenes and discuss how the different scenes are joined together. (For example, in scene 2 there are adults who seem to be the parents of the children in scene 1.)

5 Look now at the stills from the film on the next page and say how the photographs add to your knowledge of the characters. What seems to be happening in each of the photographs?

Research

1. Choose an important or memorable event from your own life to turn into a film. (It might be a stay in hospital; getting lost; a birth; marriage; celebration.) Use the script of *Hope and Glory* as a guide and write the opening scenes of your film.
   Remember to:
   a. say where the scene is, giving details of location and interior/exterior;
   b. describe what the audience will see and hear (for example, BILL *calls from the garden*);
   c. set out the dialogue like a play (for example, BILL: I thought I saw them).

2. Present a talk to your group about the way in which war is shown in films. Include, if you can, examples of films in which war is treated as:
   a. a great adventure;
   b. a comedy;
   c. an experience which makes people savage and brutal;
   d. a drama documentary, using historical characters;
   e. a fight between good (i.e. us) and bad (i.e. them);
   f. a nostalgic trip down memory lane.

   Make clear in the talk your own attitudes to war and to war films.

FILM

Stagecoach

Films (and also novels and TV programmes) can be grouped together because they are similar types or genres. Some well-known genres are: gangster films; horror; science fiction; disaster movies; musicals; comedies. Each genre has particular characteristics in terms of story, and/or setting; and/or characters.

Here are some characteristics of Westerns or cowboy films. Not every Western will have all these characteristics but it will have enough for people to call it a Western. Discuss which of the following characteristics are found in cowboy films you know.

1. They are about law and order, good and evil (in other words *goodies* and *baddies*).
2. They are set in a particular time in the past, roughly 1870–1900.
3. They are about white people settling in the west of the U.S.A.
4. They show a clash between the ideas and values of city people from the East (i.e. New York) and those of the settlers in the west.
5. They have horses.
6. They are very masculine, with a male main character, an outdoor type who hates the idea of settling down.
7. They are violent, with shooting or a chase or a fight, or all of these.
8. They have a hero who takes the law into his own hands to gain revenge.
9. They have men who treat women either brutally or with great politeness.
10. They have passive women with little to do except be protected by men. These women are either brassy bar-girls (often with hearts of gold) or quiet, virtuous city ladies who eventually adjust to western ways.
11. They show the death of many Red Indians and their way of life.
12. They celebrate noble characteristics such as courage, honesty, endurance and the will to survive.
13. They show scenes of deserts, plains and mountains.
14. They include the activities of a group of men who fight against evil only if they are given money.

Westerns have stock characters (for example, the hero or heroine; the Indian chief) who are associated with particular places, possessions and incidents. Think of some Westerns you know. Copy the chart and fill in the columns for six characters. The first line is done for you.

	Character	Place	Possession	Incident
a	The gun-fighter	saloon	six-gun	shooting after card game
b				
c				
d				
e				
f				

Here is an extract from the screenplay of the film *Stagecoach*, which appeared in 1939. It is a famous example of the Western genre. Read the extract through two or three times, as if it were a play, and then answer the questions which follow.

Cast

Buck, the driver
Curly, U.S. Marshal
Gatewood, bank manager
Peacock, whiskey salesman
Boone, drunken doctor
Dallas, saloon girl
Lucy, young army wife
Hatfield, gambler
Ringo, escaped prisoner

Close-up of BUCK and CURLY up on the driving-seat. CURLY, his gun across his knees, scans the horizon.
BUCK chucks a stone at Nellie, shouting a little to spur on the horses. He clears his throat, inviting conversation, but CURLY pays him no heed. Finally BUCK can't stand the silence and turns as if CURLY had spoken.

BUCK: What'd you say?

CURLY: (*looking at him as if he were crazy*) Nothin'.

BUCK: (*meekly*) Oh, excuse me. Well, why don't you say somethin'? A man gets nervous settin' here like a mummy, thinkin' about Indians!

(*Inside the stagecoach, the passengers are seated in the same positions as during the morning. The heat is stifling and dust drifts in through the open windows. The coach jolts and bounces as it whirls along at fourteen miles an hour. GATEWOOD is playing the indignant man-of-affairs.*)

GATEWOOD: (*blustering*) I can't get over the impertinence of that young lieutenant!
(*DOC BOONE, again with the sample bag in his lap, is very thoughtfully attempting to rearrange PEACOCK's scarf round his neck. The wind is blowing it about so much that it is a futile exercise.*)

GATEWOOD: I'll report him to Washington! We pay taxes to the government and what do we get? Not even protection from the Army! (*off*)
(*PEACOCK is now seen in close-up with DOC BOONE just in shot, his hand rearranging the scarf so that is practically covers PEACOCK's face. While GATEWOOD continues to hold forth, DOC BOONE cleans the dust from PEACOCK's face.*)

GATEWOOD: Why, they're talking now about having bank examiners . . . *he snorts* . . . as if we didn't know how to run our own banks.

(*The stagecoach is going really fast and a stiff breeze is coming through the windows. DALLAS desperately tries to rearrange her hat, which is being blown about.*
Cut back to PEACOCK and DOC BOONE, who pulls a bottle from the sample-case and holds it up to PEACOCK.
PEACOCK does not protest. So DOC BOONE takes a large swallow.)

GATEWOOD: I actually had a letter, from some official, saying they were going to inspect my books!
(*GATEWOOD now addresses his remarks to LUCY, as the most worthy of attention.*)

GATEWOOD: Don't let the government meddle with business!
(*LUCY leans agains the side of the coach, as far away from him as possible.*)

79

GATEWOOD: What the country needs is a businessman for President!
DOC BOONE: (*amiably, holding up a bottle*): What the country needs is more bottle. (*He points to the bottle.*)
PEACOCK: What?
DOC BOONE: Bottle! (*affably*)
(*DALLAS, sitting next to GATEWOOD, has her eyes closed and her head leaning against the back of the seat.*)
GATEWOOD: You're drunk, sir.
(*DOC BOONE's smile fades as he turns indignantly to GATEWOOD.*)
DOC BOONE: I'm happy, Gatewood. Woof! (*He giggles.*)
(*Now it is early evening. The stage comes into shot in the foreground, the horses trotting away down the track which stretches way into the distance across the flat desert.
Again we see CURLY and BUCK on the driving-seat, CURLY nearer to camera. He looks over his shoulder.*)

CURLY (*turning back*): How come you're using this road? It's gonna be cold up there.
BUCK: I'm using my head. Those beach-crowd Apaches don't like snow. (*grinning*)
(*CURLY looks at him, but says nothing.
In the stagecoach, the passengers are all weary, their shoulders covered with dust. LUCY, seen in medium close-up, is in obvious distress, looking very ill and worn out.
DALLAS is shown leaning back against her seat. GATEWOOD is sitting next to her with an unpleasant frown on his face and clasping his bag of money. DALLAS, who has been looking in LUCY's direction, suddenly ventures for the first time to address her. She sits up and leans sympathetically across GATEWOOD.*)
DALLAS: Wouldn't you like me to sit beside you? You could lean on my shoulder. You look so tired.
(*LUCY pulls herself together and her cool tone rebuffs DALLAS.*)
LUCY: No, thank you.
(*DALLAS shrinks back into her seat, flushing. HATFIELD, seen sitting in profile with PEACOCK nearest to camera beside him, leans forward. Camera pans left with his movement to include RINGO, who*

is sitting on the floor between the seats.)
HATFIELD: How are you feeling, Mrs Mallory?
(LUCY looks over towards DALLAS. Then she turns to HATFIELD.)
LUCY: Is there any water?
(RINGO looks at HATFIELD, HATFIELD turns away and, cupping his hand round his mouth, leans out of the window to shout up to BUCK.)
HATFIELD: Driver! Canteen, please!
(CURLY, just visible up on the box, passes a canteen down to HATFIELD, who is reaching out of the window to receive it.
LUCY can be seen leaning back wearily through the opposite window.
Inside the coach, RINGO takes the canteen and undoes the cap as HATFIELD fumbles in his jacket for something. RINGO offers the canteen to LUCY.)
HATFIELD : Just a minute, Mrs Mallory. *(off)*
(HATFIELD takes the canteen from RINGO and pours some of the water into a small silver cup, which he has in his hand.
He fills the cup, then passes it to LUCY.
LUCY takes the cup from HATFIELD's outstretched hand and gracefully drinks. Then she closes its little lid and looks at it as if trying to recall something from her memory. She then looks up at HATFIELD and leans forward, pointing to the cup as she questions him.)
LUCY: Haven't I seen this crest before? *(Holding out the cup)* Isn't this from Ringfield Manor?
(HATFIELD takes the cup.)
HATFIELD: I wouldn't know, Mrs Mallory. I won that cup on a wager.
(LUCY seems disappointed by his reply. RINGO, sitting in his position on the floor, breaks the silence.)
RINGO *(looking up at HATFIELD)*: How about the other lady?
(DALLAS is lying back against the headrest with her eyes closed, next to GATEWOOD. He looks down disapprovingly. She slowly opens her eyes and looks up with a grateful smile.
RINGO takes the canteen from HATFIELD's extended hand, pulls off the cork and offers it up towards DALLAS.)
DALLAS: Thanks.
(RINGO's eyes flick across towards HATFIELD, then, still grinning, he passes the canteen over to DALLAS.)
RINGO: Sorry – no silver cup.
(DALLAS leans forward a little to take it.)
DALLAS *(quickly)*: This is fine. *(She raises the canteen to her lips. GATEWOOD watches her disapprovingly as she drinks deeply from it. Then with a pleasant smile she offers him the canteen.)*
GATEWOOD *(shaking his head in disgust)*: No!
(DALLAS looks down towards RINGO, smiles bravely and hands him back the canteen.)

1. Which of the fourteen characteristics of a Western listed earlier seem to fit *Stagecoach*?
2. Talk about the characters in the extract and try to match them with the figures shown in the still(s).
3. The plot of *Stagecoach* uses a very old way to tell its story. It brings together a group of different people, puts them in a confined space (the stagecoach itself) and sends them on a journey. As they travel we learn about their lives and characters. At least three of these passengers are outsiders from respectable society. Who are they? How do we know they are outsiders? What hints are there in the scene of how the three characters might 'save' themselves, become accepted by the other passengers, or help the group to survive?
4. There are nine people in the extract. Choose two of them and, building on the details in the extract, invent a brief biography for each one. Include details of their characters; important events in their lives and backgrounds, and say how they came to be in the coach that day.
5. In another part of the film:
   a Ringo stops the coach on its way to Lordsburg;
   b Dallas urges Ringo to escape;
   c The group votes whether or not to go on, when faced with the Apache threat.
   Choose one of these incidents and write the screenplay for it, combining dialogue with description, as in the extract.

Research

1. Think about other film genres, such as Science Fiction; Musical; Horror; Gangster; Comedy; History. Choose one of these genres and list its characteristics (as we have done for the Western). Write a detailed account of one film you know well, showing how it fits the genre.
2. Not all modern films fit the genres listed in Question 1. Talk about some films you have seen recently and decide on a genre for them.

FILM

Very Special Effects

Butch Cassidy and the Sundance Kid leap hundreds of feet into a raging river; James Bond fights under water; the *Titanic* sinks; King Kong towers above the New York skyline and swats aeroplanes. How is it all done? How do the actors survive?

The answers lie in the tricks of the film trade. This Unit describes a number of special effects and how they are achieved. First, a summary of many of them, in the form of a poem.

Horror Film

Well sir, first of all there was this monster
But like he's not really a monster
'Cause in real life he's a bank clerk sir
And sings in this village choir
But he keeps like drinking this potion sir
And you see him like changing into this pig
With black curly hairs on his knuckles;
And what he does sir,
Is he goes round eating people's brains.
Anyway before that sir, I should have said
He's secretly in love with Lady Irene
Who's very rich with lots of long frocks
And she has this identical twin sister
Who looks like her sir
Who keeps getting chased by this monster bulldog
Into these sinking sands
That's inhabited by this prehistoric squid sir
Which like she can't see
Because the deaf and dumb bailiff
With the hump on his back
Has trod on her specs.
Anyway before that sir,
I should have said,
This Lady Irene is screaming,
'Henry, Henry, my beloved, save me,'
'Cause she's been walled up in the dripping dungeon
With the mad violinist of the vaults
By the manservant with the withered boot sir.
But this Henry, he can't hear her sir,
Because he's too busy
Putting people in this bubbling acid bath
To make them stay young forever sir
But his experiments keep going wrong.
Anyway, before that sir,
I should have said,
Her Dad can't rescue her either sir
Because of the army of giant ants
That's eating his castle;

And the music sir, it's going,
'Tarrar, tarrar, boom boom tarrar sir,'
And 'Henry, Henry my beloved,'
She keeps screaming
And the mad violinist of the vaults sir
He starts going funny all over the flagstones.
And like, Algernon sir,
No not him sir, the other one,
He can't do nothing about the squid in the bogs
Because he's turning into this pig with hairy knuckles.
Anyway before that sir, I should have said,
There's this huge mummy in the library
And every time he hears this music
Starts tearing off all these dirty bandages
And smashing through these walls and everything
And the professor can't stop him
'Cause he's gone off his rocker
And keeps bulging his eyes and laughing a lot
When suddenly this vampire . . .
Didn't I tell you about the vampire sir?
Anyway before that there's this vampire
Who's been dead for thousands of years
But he's a Swiss greengrocer in real life
But the iceberg his coffin's in
Gets all broken up sir
When it collides with Dr Strenkhoff's submarine sir,
That's carrying this secret cargo
Of radio active rats . . .
Didn't I tell you about the radio active rats sir?
Well anyway sir
Before that I should have said . . .

Gareth Owen

1 Practise reading this poem out loud, as if you were a young boy or girl telling your teacher.

2 List the special effects it describes, starting with the bank clerk becoming a monster.

Memoirs of Frankenstein

By Boris Karloff

It is not true that I was born a monster. Hollywood made me one. My big break came while I was downing a sandwich-and-tea lunch. Someone tapped me on the shoulder and said, 'Mr. Whale would like to see you at his table.' Jimmy Whale was the most important director on the lot. 'We're getting ready to shoot the Mary Shelley classic, *Frankenstein*,' Whale said, 'and I'd like you to test – for the monster.'

It was a bit shattering, but I felt that any part was better than no part at all. The studio's head make-up man, Jack Pierce, spent evenings experimenting with me. Slowly, under his skilful touch, the monster's double-domed forehead, sloping brow, flattened Neanderthal eyelids and surgical scars materialized. A week later I was ready for the test. I readily passed as a monster.

The scene where the monster was created, amid booming and thunder and flashing lightning, made me as uneasy as anyone. For while I lay half-naked and strapped to Doctor Frankenstein's table, I could see directly above me the special-effects men brandishing the white-hot scissorslike carbons that made the lightning. I hoped that no one up there had butterfingers.

Frankenstein finally was released for its premiere on December 6, 1931, at Santa Barbara. I was not even invited and had never seen it. I was just an unimportant freelance actor, the animation for the monster costume.

Frankenstein transformed not only my life but also the film industry. It grossed something like $12 million on a $250,000 investment, started a cycle of so-called boy-meets-ghoul horror films and quickly made its producers realize they'd made a dreadful mistake. They let the monster die in the burning mill. In one brief script conference, however, they brought him back alive. It seems he had only fallen through the flaming floor into the pond and could now go on for reels and reels.

Boris played the immortal monster only three times and became irrevocably identified as Frankenstein thereafter.

1 How does Boris Karloff seem to feel about Frankenstein in terms of:
   a the way the part changed his life?
   b the make-up and special effects needed?
   c the profits made by the film?

2 Write a piece of free verse entitled, *From Me to Monster*, or a piece of prose commentary putting down the thoughts that go through Karloff's head as he is made up for yet another Frankenstein film.

Models

For one of his many effects on *Superman, The Movie*, Derek Meddings designed a huge miniature of the Golden Gate Bridge, which straddled the giant water tank at Pinewood. His effects team crashed model cars on the model roadway of the bridge, but most viewers assume they are watching full-scale crashes. For *Superman II*, Meddings designed a superbly detailed model of the Eiffel Tower for the opening sequence and a vast miniature of 42nd Street on which, again, he crashed model cars and caused minature mayhem. Here audiences believe they are watching events on a full-size street because Meddings moved model pedestrians along the sidewalks in the background. For the scenes at the villain's headquarters in *The Spy Who Loved Me* (1977), he used moving model guards and miniature helicopters to confuse the viewers' sense of scale.

Meddings' miniature work on scenes involving explosions and water is remarkable because neither fire nor water can be realistically scaled-down. To overcome this on *The Spy Who Loved Me*, he designed a 63-foot-long, 12-ton, 'miniature' oil-tanker, fitted with water disturbers on the hull, which he filmed and sank at sea off the Bahamas.

Glass painting

A waterfall panorama created by Les Bowie for Hammer's *When Dinosaurs Ruled the Earth* (1970). The background is a painting on glass. The cliffs are polystyrene. The figures are live actors but they are not in front of the camera. The background has a mirror inset that reflects the actors – who are standing in another part of the studio. Nothing, therefore, is real.

1 Talk in your group about some films you have seen where small-scale models were used for particular effects. Did you realise at the time that models were being used?

2 What other effects could you achieve using the technique of painting on glass? You might think about:
   a   large battle formations
   b   landscapes
   c   fire and smoke
   d   scenes in space

Laboratory work

When the script calls for a sequence on the leaf-cutter ant, or the inside of a termite mound, or the behaviour of a small fish on the river-bed, these will more than likely have to be filmed under artificial conditions. Reptiles, fish and insects can be flown thousands of miles from their native habitat and encouraged to go about their normal business in the seclusion of a laboratory. This sort of highly-detailed work makes it possible for David Attenborough to illustrate many points about animals that simply cannot be made in the wild.

1 Talk about some surprising shots in wild life films you have seen, involving insects or animals or fish. Choose shots which could only have been achieved in a laboratory or by careful arrangement, but which seem in the film to have taken place in the wild.

Sound track (*Star Wars*)

We now have an enormous library of explosion noises – more than 160 of them – which is certainly more than we would ever need. But I keep on searching for the ultimate explosion. The raw material for the laser bolts and the weaponry sound effects in *Star Wars* came from a variety of sources. I made expeditions to places like artillery firing ranges and missile bases just to collect sounds. Sometimes we'll hire real weapons just to record the sound of them firing and occasionally, we'll mess around with quarter-pound blocks of TNT or blow up holes in hillsides or explode trees or junked automobiles. Orchestrating an explosion, especially a big one, is a fine art and I've been experimenting with the sounds by mixing in horns and shrieks and bells to give them more variety. The big thing is, you don't just want them to go BOOOOOM.

It's always the most unexpected that's the most interesting. I went to the White Sands missile testing range once in search of good missile engine sounds. I got a lot of different missile sounds but they weren't nearly as interesting in the end as the air conditioner in the motel where I was staying. It was malfunctioning in my room and producing a very good throb. You might find it hard to believe, but that throb has been useful in constructing many of the large ship noises in all the *Star Wars* movies.

Visual effects

Supervising the visual effects on any *Star Wars* movie presents problems.

On *Return of the Jedi* we have literally had our cameras going 24 hours a day with a day crew and a night crew with both crews working six days a week. On *The Empire Strikes Back*, for example, we produced 1,650 camera reports. (Every time an element is shot, it is accompanied by a camera report.) For *Return of the Jedi*, we will almost certainly produce 3,000 cam reports and our filing system has been put on a computer.

For a single shot that might last a second or two on screen, involving two dozen spaceships in formation or battling it out, we are working with as many as fifty-seven separate elements. This means fifty-seven separate pieces of film, fifty-six for the ships themselves and a final element for the starfield. George Lucas personally approved every single element. Not just every shot, but every element – every ship, every planet, every laserburst.

The only stock shots we can resort to is to go back to *The Empire Strikes Back* and *Star Wars* and use stuff like starfields and ships that didn't appear in the final print. So, another part of our job is to keep track of all that film, or the elements, from all the previous movies and often I'll spend days researching such material. Of course, the fans would never be able to tell from which particular movie a particular starfield or a shot of a ship might have come because we make sure that the ships are re-positioned, turned upside down and changed in any number of ways.

1 These extracts about sound track and visual effects tell us about how these effects were achieved. They also tell us a lot about the job done by a special effects person and the qualities needed for that job. Assuming you could work either on sound track, or visual effects, as described in these extracts, which would you choose and why?

2 Drawing upon the information given in the extracts say how you think the following special effects are achieved?
   a a person being crushed by falling rocks
   b the sound of thunder
   c walking across a tightrope strung between two skyscrapers
   d cars exploding and bursting into flames over a cliff edge
   e Superman flying
   f wind and rain, with lightning flashes
   g battling through fire or water
   h being trampled under horses' hooves

Research

1 Analyse carefully a video-clip advertising a pop song or pop star and make a list of all the special effects it achieves. Which, do you think, are the most effective, and why?

2 Describe in precise detail, for the benefit of someone who has not seen it, a very special effect achieved by a stunt man or stunt woman in any film you know.

3 One special effect in the *Star Wars* films was the creation of several languages, either for creatures or robots. Write a short piece, with English translation, in which you invent a language to describe:
   a a marvellous sporting event you witnessed;
   b the reception of a pop star by thousands of fans;
   c a car factory operated by robots.

BRIEFING

People Grading

People in advertising and marketing need to know their targets, the consumers they are aiming at. Few teenagers are interested in pensions; no vegetarian in beefburgers; no eleven year old in the Government's latest tax changes.

One way of identifying markets is to use a system of grouping people according to the job of the head of household (that is, the person in the family who earns most money). Here is one widely-used system.

Social grades in the UK		
Grade	Occupation of head of household	Percentage of population
A	Top managers, administrators and professionals (e.g. the director of a public company, a senior civil servant, surgeon)	3.1
B	Middle managers, administrators and professionals (e.g. a works manager, the head of a secondary school)	13.4
C1	Supervisors, office staff (e.g. a senior secretary, teacher)	22.3
C2	Skilled manual (e.g. a motor engineer, a rail driver)	31.2
D	Semi-skilled and unskilled manual (e.g. a coal-miner, a shop assistant)	19.1
E	Those with the lowest standard of living (e.g. casual labourers, pensioners, widows, unemployed)	10.9

1. As you talk about this table, discuss:
   a. Where you would place a toolmaker; doctor; computer programmer; architect; crossing warden; Member of Parliament.
   b. Whether people can or should be slotted into a social class in this way.

2. Also discuss which grades (A, B, C1, C2, D, E) you would aim at and why, in advertising and marketing these products:
   - fish fingers
   - Austin Rover cars
   - golf umbrellas
   - skin cream
   - health food
   - tents
   - cable TV
   - new magazine for basketball

   Which products did you have difficulty in grading? Why was this?

3. Finally, look carefully at the following chart which shows the favourite television programmes, by social class, of a (small) sample of 793 people.

   a Who dislikes variety shows, game shows and news?
   b Who particularly likes wildlife programmes, feature films, situation comedies and soap operas?
   c Are these results more or less what you would expect, or do they surprise you in any way? How reliable do you think they are? (What might make them unreliable?)

	Favourite TV Programmes				
	Total	Class			
		AB	C1	C2	DE
Weighted base	793	128	219	215	231
	%	%	%	%	%
Soap operas	29	22	28	32	33
Situation comedies	29	30	29	34	24
Other comedy programmes	16	19	14	18	16
Variety shows	9	1	10	7	15
Quiz shows	25	15	19	27	36
Sports	28	28	22	28	32
News	15	23	25	6	8
Wildlife programmes	39	31	37	45	38
Documentaries	32	50	30	34	21
Feature films	42	36	47	42	39
Game shows	8	4	5	6	15
Chat shows	10	16	10	6	11
Travel programmes	12	19	15	8	9
Religious programmes	1	2	–	–	–
Other	2	3	2	2	1
Don't know/no answer	1	–	1	1	–

BRIEFING

Legal, Decent, Honest, Truthful?

For many years advertising was not controlled at all. For example, in the 1890s Bovril used the Pope in its advertisements (without his permission). Other adverts claimed that cigarettes cured sore throats and that alcohol was good for you.

In the 1960s the public was suddenly faced with a greater range of goods than ever before. People realised that some controls were needed to stop misleading advertisements. The advertising industry itself drew up its own Code of Practice. This is now supervised by the Advertising Standards Authority (A.S.A.). This body can:
- ask advertisers to stop publishing offending adverts;
- give offenders bad publicity;
- investigate people's complaints and check them against its Code of Practice.

The A.S.A. cannot:
- force advertisers to change their adverts;

It does not:
- cover TV and radio adverts.

According to the A.S.A. Code of Practice, adverts should be Legal, Decent, Honest and Truthful.

Legal
1. Adverts should not contain anything that is against the law.
2. They should not encourage people to break the law.

Decent
1. Adverts should not include indecent or offensive material.
2. They should not promote certain beliefs or opinions in such a way as to offend groups of people.

Honest
1. Adverts should not take advantage of people's lack of experience or knowledge.
2. They should be written in such a way that the meaning is clear.

Truthful
1. Adverts should not mislead people in any way. Advertisers can give opinions but should have good evidence for any statements of fact they make.
2. Advertisers should not advertise products unless they are sure they can meet the demand.

IF AN ADVERT IS WRONG, WHO PUTS IT RIGHT?

We do.

The Advertising Standards Authority ensures advertisements meet with the strict Code of Advertising Practice. So if you question an advertiser, they have to answer to us.

To find out more about the ASA, please write to Advertising Standards Authority, Dept. X, Brook House, Torrington Place, London WC1E 7HN.

ASA

This space is donated in the interests of high standards in advertisements.

The Code states that advertisements:
1. should be fair and responsible;
2. should not play on fear, without a good reason (such as encouraging people to behave better);
3. should not show or support dangerous behaviour (except in the cause of safety).

The Code also covers other areas in great detail, such as:
a alcohol
b slimming
c cigarettes and tobacco
d children
e hair and scalp products
f mail order
g financial services

1. Discuss what you have learnt so far about the A.S.A. and whether or not you think it performs a useful function in our society.

2. Think about the areas **a** to **g** and the ways in which advertisers in these areas might offend against the Code. Make notes on each of these possible offences for **c** to **g**. The first two, **a** and **b**, are done for you.

   a Alcohol
   Adverts should not encourage excessive drinking, such as the repeated buying of large rounds. Adverts can suggest the pleasure of having company while drinking, but should not suggest that a drink can help sexual success or make the drinker more attractive to the opposite sex.

   b Slimming
   Claims that you can lose up to X pounds, look X pounds lighter, start to slim in X days, lose X inches immediately, etc. should not be made since the weights and measurements of different people vary too much. So advertisers cannot keep these promises. Also adverts should not suggest that slimming methods cannot fail. They should not claim to treat overweight people who really need medical attention.

3. Here and on pages 90 and 91, are some complaints about certain adverts which have broken a part of the Code. Decide in each case which area of the Code has been broken, that is, the area relating to:

a	Legality	e	Children
b	Decency	f	Alcohol
c	Honesty	g	Slimming
d	Truth		

   Choose two of the adverts which have broken the Code and, in the role of an A.S.A. official, write a short report on each to the advertisers in order to:
   - explain that you have received a complaint;
   - state which part of the Code has been broken;
   - give your reasons for supporting the complaint;
   - tell the advertisers what they should do to correct the advert.

A charity organisation complains of:

'A national press advertisement for the Sprite Turbo HC which was headlined 'Hot from the Start' and continued......... 'the fastest road car yet......... A 2.2 engine gives the Sprite even more muscle.......... Faster than a Porsche and leaving even Ferrari waiting.......... race-bred handling.' It was captioned, 'Race Bred For the Road.'

Programmes for the treatment of **Cellulite & Obesity**

NEW YEAR OFFER

Shed those ugly lumps and bumps
GUARANTEED weight and inch
loss fast and easy
the **21ST CENTURY** way
or your money back

Mr P. of Liverpool writes:

I saw a cinema advertisement for Bill Crockett's Southern Whiskey. In it a man took a woman to a bar in a night club. They were supposed to have had a row and were meeting in the friendly atmosphere of the local bar. The woman looked into the man's eyes on being given the glass of whiskey. The row then seemed to be over. Finally, the couple were seen dancing in dimmed lighting in a close embrace.

Mr B. of Newcastle writes:

I saw an advertisement for a department store's winter sale which said, 'Sheepskin Bargains. Men's three-quarter length. Half-price. £200, now £99.' I visited the store at the opening of the first day of the sale but was told there were no three-quarter length men's sheepskin coats in the sale. Why, then, were these coats included in the advertisement?

£100 'cheque' - but only if you move house

A woman from Leeds objected to an envelope, delivered by hand, which stated '£100 cheque enclosed'. When she opened the envelope, she found it was promoting a local estate agent, and what the 'cheque' actually allowed her was a discount of £100 against the estate agent's normal fees. According to the estate agent, the 'cheque' met the definition of a cheque.

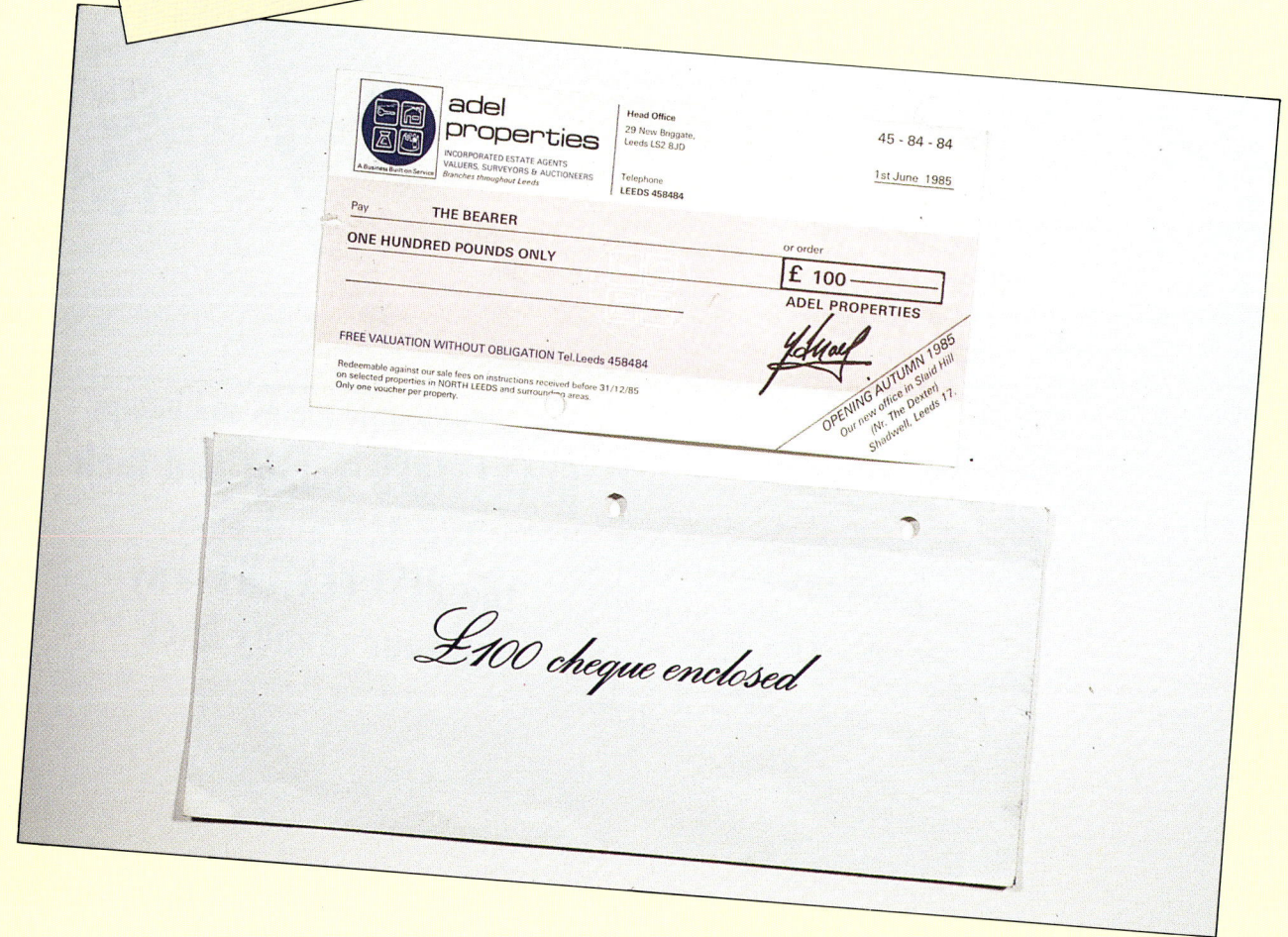

A child care organisation objected to this press advertisement.

Mr A. of Bristol writes:

An advertisement in the front of the Meat Trades Journal for natural sausage casings included a photograph of a female model and read, 'Hello. Natural skin time again. I was born with mine, but my butcher gets his from experts.'

Ms P. of Glasgow says:

A national press advert for Magneton 5 and Gold Magneton Body Spray claimed, 'Do you attract women? Here's the answer. Create instant magnetism. Girls can't resist it. Featured on TV. Blondes and Redheads noticed Magneton 5 more quickly than others. Gold Magneton 4, specially for you girls to get the blokes running after you. You wear it at your own risk.' Are these products really effective?

BRIEFING

Reading the Small Print

British newspapers depend on advertisers – their only other source of income being the cover price paid by the readers.

One very valuable form of advertising, particularly with local papers, is the classified advertising from private individuals or small businesses announcing births, deaths and marriages, services and goods for sale and so on.

Here is the index of classified advertisements used in a local paper:

200 PROPERTY & LAND FOR SALE
- 200 PROPERTY AND LAND FOR SALE
- 201 PROPERTY AND LAND WANTED
- 202 ACCOMMODATION AND PROPERTY TO LET
- 203 BUSINESS FOR SALE
- 204 BUSINESS WANTED
- 205 COMMERCIAL
- 206 AUCTIONS AND ANTIQUES

300 ANNOUNCEMENTS
- 300 PUBLIC NOTICES
- 301 RELIGIOUS NOTICES
- 302 BIRTHS
- 303 ENGAGEMENTS
- 304 MARRIAGES
- 305 DEATHS
- 306 IN MEMORIA
- 307 THANKS
- 308 CONGRATULATIONS
- 309 EXAM RESULTS
- 310 ANNIVERSARIES
- 311 BIRTHDAY GREETINGS
- 312 WEDDINGS
- 313 LOST AND FOUND
- 314 CHRISTMAS GREETINGS
- 315 FUNERAL DIRECTORS
- 316 GET WELL
- 317 GOOD LUCK
- 318 FLORAL TRIBUTES
- 319 ACKNOWLEDGEMENTS
- 320 BIRTHDAY MEMORIES

400 FOR SALE AND WANTS
- 400 ARTICLES FOR SALE
- 401 WANTED
- 402 PERSONAL
- 403 MOTHER AND BABY
- 404 HEALTH AND BEAUTY
- 405 NURSING HOMES
- 406 RESIDENTIAL AND REST HOMES
- 407 PETS
- 408 HORSE AND RIDING
- 409 LIVESTOCK & FARMER
- 410 MUSICAL INSTRUMENTS
- 411 BOATS
- 412 CAMPING/CARAVANS
- 413 OFFICE EQUIPMENT
- 414 ELECTRICAL

500 SERVICES
- 500 HOME SERVICES
- 501 HEATING & PLUMBING
- 502 DECORATIVE
- 503 GLAZING
- 504 ROOFING
- 505 INSULATION
- 506 PLASTERING
- 507 CARPENTRY & JOINERY
- 508 ELECTRICAL & APPLIANCES
- 509 AERIAL INSTALLATION
- 510 FIREPLACES & CANOPIES
- 511 SECURITY
- 512 RADIO/TV/VIDEO
- 513 COMPUTERS
- 514 GARDENING
- 515 WASTE DISPOSAL
- 516 FOR HIRE
- 517 REMOVALS & STORAGE
- 518 PLANT & MACHINERY
- 519 HAULAGE
- 520 DISTRIBUTION
- 521 PROMOTIONAL PUBLICITY
- 522 PRINTING
- 523 PROFESSIONAL & BUSINESS SERVICES
- 524 PLANNING SERVICES
- 525 FINANCE & INSURANCE
- 526 TUITION
- 527 CATERING
- 528 PIANO TUNING
- 529 PHOTOGRAPHY
- 530 WATCH AND CLOCK REPAIRS
- 531 MEDICAL SERVICES
- 532 PRIVATE HEALTH CARE
- 533 ANTIQUES
- 534 FURNITURE STRIPPING/RENOVATIONS
- 535 CARPETS
- 536 UPHOLSTERY/FURNISHINGS

600 HOLIDAYS
- 600 HOLIDAYS

700 EMPLOYMENT
- 701 SITUATIONS VACANT
- 702 PART-TIME VACANCIES
- 703 SITUATIONS WANTED

800 MOTORS
- 800 CARS FOR SALE
- 801 CARS WANTED
- 802 MOTORCYCLES/CYCLES
- 803 COMMERCIAL VEHICLES
- 804 SPARES/ACCESSORIES
- 805 REPAIRS/SERVICING
- 806 MOTOR INSURANCE
- 807 DRIVING TUITION
- 808 VEHICLE HIRE
- 809 CAR DISMANTLERS

Professional Confectioner offers

Cake-a-Gram

Novelty cakes decorated to your design, complete with card, your place, your time

Telephone 26678

Weddings, anniversaries, birthdays and special occasions.

MAESTRO Roof Rack, genuine BL unused, still in box. offers Tel. 78770 (evenings)

SHORT CUTS

Mobile Hairdresser

Tel: Mandy 5260

QUALITY GROOMING & TRIMMIMG

For all breeds of dogs and cross breeds

Ring Sheila

Telephone 872049

Records wanted

LPs, singles, CDs, tapes, old pop magazines etc. Any age any quantity Ring Mister Tee on 6845 for details

---

ACUPUNCTURE CAN HELP YOU STOP SMOKING * REDUCE WEIGHT

Relief from:

PAIN, TENSION, MIGRAINE, ANXIETY, PERIOD PAINS, DEPRESSION, ARTHRITIS, PANIC, RHEUMATISM, STRESS, BACK PAINS, INSOMNIA

Acupuncture is a system of medicine which is used to restore and maintain good health, as well as in the prevention of illness.

It is painless, without side effects and has an excellent success rate.

Ring now for an early appointment

Mr and Mrs E. Thompson are happy to announce the engagement on Dec. 26th of their daughter Ann-Marie to Martin, only son of Mr and Mrs W. Legat of Broom Hill. Love and congratulations from both families.

---

1. Using this index how would you classify the following ads? For each one decide on the most appropriate index number (200 – 810).

2. Write and design a small ad for an article you want to sell.

Sheds, Summer Houses, Solar Sheds and Conservatories

STRONG WELL MADE SHEDS

All sizes available, windows and door positions to suit you. Complete with floor, roof felted, glass fitted.

SPECIAL OFFER

8 ft x 6 ft PENT £160 **delivered inc VAT**

Visit our display site and see a large range of SHEDS, SUMMER HOUSES, SOLAR SHEDS, GREENHOUSES and ALUMINIUM or uPVC CONSERVATORIES BACO, CRITTALL, WESSEX, EDEN, AGL & ATNAF

Open Monday to Saturday 9 am to 5 pm, Sunday 9 am to 12 noon

TELEPHONE ORDERS WELCOME 03721

SPRING '89 COURSES
RECREATIONAL COURSES AT STOURMINSTER COLLEGE

Put your spare time to good use in the New Year. We have vacancies on the following part-time day and evening courses commencing Tuesday, January 3, 1989.

- Dressmaking
- Pottery
- Art
- Flower arranging/Floristry
- Ladies Keep-Fit
- Soft Furnishing
- Mens Keep-Fit
- Children's Wear
- Tatting
- Multi-Gym
- Beginners Guitar
- Intermediate Guitar
- Badminton
- Yoga
- Hostess Cookery
- Woodwork
- Music
- Bobbin Lace
- Fabric & Paper Flower Making
- Matures Photography

Enrolment for the above courses takes place at Stourminster College on January 3, 4 and 5, 1989 at 6.30 — 7.30 pm

---

MERCHANDISER
Location South England

- This is a unique opportunity to commence a first class selling career merchandising our products in Retail Outlets in the South of England.
- This opportunity will allow the successful applicant to learn the skills of merchandising and sales with the possibility of promotion at a later date to the established sales team. Applicants possibly having some experience in Sales and Marketing should be keen self starters, fit and preferably with an artistic flair. A clean driving licence is essential.
- Reporting to the Marketing Manager you will be responsible for merchandising instore and window displays and assisting the area Sales Representative.
- A good salary, company van and the usual benefits of a large company await the successful applicant.
- **Applications with CV to: Mr R. B. Potter, Personnel Manager.**

NORTON STRAY FUND

We always have a selection of dogs needing permanent, caring homes.
Mrs Bardsley 50914

TYPING SERVICES

For all your typing requirements small or large

Tel: 44283

24hr Ans service

DANIELS— Happy 39th Birthday, Peter Pan. I love you. From your very own BONG.

DOSANJH —Pritpal, Congratulations on passing your exams. Love Mum and Dad.

TELEPHONE DATING ☎

Ring in now and listen to girls who want to meet guys

GUYS LISTEN TO GIRLS

Research

1. Make a study of, and write a report on, the advertisements carried by several different newspapers. Compare them in terms of:
   - **amount** of advertising, as a proportion of the paper as a whole;
   - **type** of advertisement (What is being advertised, size of ad, design, colour, boxed display?);
   - **target reader** (Who is the advertisement aimed at? For example, the general public, people in one area, a particular type of person with regard to age, sex, social group?)

2. Compare the advertising carried by different types of magazine. For this use:
   - a magazine aimed primarily at teenage girls;
   - a magazine aimed primarily at women;
   - a specialist magazine, for example, on cars or computers or sport.

   Present your findings in the form of a display or a report for your group.

BRIEFING

Good News

The view taken in this Unit is that TV news is often presented as entertainment. Read on and see whether you agree or disagree with this view.

Where does your knowledge of the news come from?
62% of the population gets its information from television;
23% from newspapers;
13% from radio.

Is the sole task of a TV news broadcast to convey information, or is it supposed to do other things as well? In fact, do such broadcasts provide more entertainment than information?

Think about the following points and try to answer some of the questions:

The Music

News broadcasts are introduced by exciting, familiar music, as are all other shows on television.
- Why do we need music to go with the News?
- What is the effect when there is an occasional bulletin which has no music?

The News-readers

News-readers are often good-looking and friendly, with an air of authority.
- Why don't they tend to be fat, ugly, cross-eyed, or lacking in confidence?

Look at the following photographs and choose the best as a TV news-reader.

They sit behind desks.
- Why?

They react little to stories, even though these may concern tragedy, brutality.
- Why not?

They often read the news in pairs.
- Why?

The tabloid papers treat news-readers as celebrities and write about their private lives and high salaries. Television companies poach popular news-readers from each other.
- Are news-readers more important than the news itself?

News-reader or News-presenter or News-caster?
- Which is the better name and why?

The Presentation

However serious a news item may be, it will be followed by advertisements on commercial stations or by an informal weather forecast on BBC. Imagine the effect on your mind of reading a serious book punctuated by advertisements or jokes.
- What is the effect on the viewer of having news stories followed quickly by advertisements?

News items are very short, with an average length of forty-five seconds. This means that important items may get three or four minutes of coverage; minor items under 30 seconds.
- How does this affect the coverage of complex issues?

Short items with films and computer graphics help viewers to concentrate longer.
- Does this stop people from thinking about what they have seen, or does it help understanding by taking viewers through complicated stories?

There is a proportion of *soft* (that is, trivial) items in each broadcast. Often at the end of the news, they may concern the Royal Family, or animals, and take up more time than important stories.
- What is good and bad about including *soft* items?

After a tragedy cameras often linger on, or show close-up views of, grief-stricken people. Also, there may be interviews which include searching, personal questions, such as: 'How do you feel now that your son/daughter/husband/wife has been attacked/murdered/imprisoned/found?'
- Should such coverage be included in news bulletins?

The news programme has to appear each night, whether or not anything really important has happened.
- What effect does this have on the items chosen?

Make Your Own News Programme

For this section you need to imagine you are the editor in charge of a late evening's bulletin. You have to decide which fifteen items will be included for the twenty-five minute bulletin and how long each will be. Choose your items from the list headed *News Stories* but before you begin, here are some points to remember:

Sequence

a Items will appear roughly in the order of hard news (politics, disasters); information (reports, new products, court cases); magazine items (Royal Family, pop stars); sport.
b The longest items (about 3 minutes) generally come first.
c The commercial channels split their bulletins into two sections with advertisements, so there may be two long items.
d The main bulletin begins with about five headlines (called *bongs*) to whet the appetite of the viewer.
e There will be some home news and some foreign news. Critics say British television reports trivial home items rather than overseas events.
f A *soft* item often ends the broadcast.

(**Note:** for this exercise, ignore the question of costs.)

1 Choose now your fifteen items from this list of news stories and decide on the length of each story and the order the stories will come in.

News stories

The American President tries to re-build his image (satellite link).
Influence of the President's wife in the White House.
A Royal Prince looks at some pandas.
Wall Street stock market record.
Flood in West Germany.
Prime Minister at economic council meeting.
Illegal payments to football players.
Pop star announces 'Say "No" to drugs'.
Princess attends Charity awards ceremony.
Soccer results.
Danish oil tanker in difficulty off English coast.
Report on City corruption.
Nazi war criminal in United States.
Nobel prize winner gets special award.
Drugs baron held in South America.
Big trade union accepts pay offer.
Fashion designers and theft.
British Telecom criticised.
Prime Minister comments on possible arms deal.

2 Write the headlines (*bongs*) for your five main stories.
3 Write the script for three of the items which will appear in your twenty-five minute broadcast.
   Here are some points to help you:
   a After the headline the first sentence tells viewers what the item is about. (For example, The Prime Minister continued talks today with the President of the United States.)
   b More detail is given about where the event took place; who was there; why they were there; what they said. (Outside reporters may do this on film.)
   c A final sentence ties up any loose ends.
4 With a partner tape-record or video the reading of the headlines and the three stories. How could your reading be improved?

Research

1 Choose one topic to investigate from those discussed earlier in the Unit.
   - Music
   - News-reader
   - Presentation
   Watch two main evening news bulletins on different channels and make notes on how your chosen topic is treated. Write a report or prepare a talk from your notes.

2 Watch two main channel news bulletins for one evening. Time each item and decide whether it was *soft* or *hard*. Compare the proportion of soft and hard items which each channel shows and the place and order in which they are shown. What conclusions do you come to?

3 Over a few weeks collect some articles on news-readers from tabloid newspapers and magazines. Make notes for a report on what is said about their:
   - Audience appeal
   - Professionalism
   - Personal lives
   Comment also on the kind of language that is used about them and on the attitudes towards them of the journalists.

BRIEFING

Planning a Documentary

In this Unit you are asked to plan a ten-minute documentary film to illustrate the work of the *National Society for the Prevention of Cruelty to Children.* (NSPCC)

Follow these stages in order.

Stage 1   Background

To begin with you need to know something about the organisation. Read the information given below. It is taken from an NSPCC leaflet and explains how the society hopes to achieve its ideal: 'to provide the means of improving the child's home life and encourage loving relationships between parents and children.'

How will we do this?

- By providing day care facilities for children and parents, because we know that expert counselling and treatment can cut the number of children being injured and neglected. We have seen whole families re-united and frightened children given a new and secure start in life after receiving skilled help at NSPCC day care centres.

- By offering practical help to parents who simply cannot handle running a home, bringing up children and coping with financial, marital and domestic burdens.

- By setting up a practical programme preparing young people for the task of being parents and implementing it through schools and youth groups.

- By offering support, advice and training to child welfare professionals; pooling our knowledge and experience for the good of the children.

- By conducting a campaign of public education and research on the causes and effects of child abuse.

- By continuing to encourage local and central government to give priority to the needs of children and campaigning for changes in the law.

- By continuing to respond at any time to any crisis in the home that might result in a child being abused or neglected.

It's an ambitious undertaking - but we can achieve it with your help. Remember we are NOT a government body. Our work depends almost entirely on the generosity of people like you. If that generosity stopped - so could we. And there are too many children at risk for that to be allowed to happen.

To help you to remember them, make a note of each of these points, putting them as briefly as you can into your own words.

Stage 2 The Idea

The idea you are going to use in this documentary is to illustrate one particular case from the files of the NSPCC.

Here is the case.

Re-building a family

Mr Gates referred himself to the Society, after his wallet was stolen. He had no other money on which to feed his three young children.

An NSPCC Child Protection Officer visited Mr Gates with food, and Mr Gates reluctantly allowed the officer into the house. The officer was shocked by the conditions he found. Peter, aged 4, and his brother John, aged 2, were sitting naked in the living room. Rose, a baby of 10 months, was lying on a broken down chair covered in a filthy blanket.

John and Peter were the same size, even though Peter was two years older than his brother. Peter appeared to be seriously underweight for his age.

The whole flat smelt of excreta and urine. The children's bedroom, which contained one single bed, was caked in excreta. The window was boarded over, with no natural light in the room. The toilet was broken. There appeared to be no clean clothes in the house, or toys for the children. The kitchen was filthy, and the only food to be seen was powdered baby milk and a few mouldy biscuits.

Immediate action was taken to protect the children. The children were medically examined, and a care order was later granted by the court, and the children were placed with foster parents.

The NSPCC made an assessment of the family, and found that when Mrs Gates had moved out of the house for several weeks following an argument, Mr Gates had been unable to cope. Even when Mrs Gates had returned home, the condition of the house and the care of the children had not improved. There had been serious difficulties in their marital relationship for some time, and the children had become pawns in their parents' continuous squabbling. They had been subjected to severe physical neglect, and were listless and nervous.

Both parents recognised that they had failed to care properly for their children, and the NSPCC officer worked with them to improve the conditions in the home, and their ability to look after their children. The parents were also helped to deal more constructively with their marital problems.

The conditions in the home gradually improved, and the children were returned home on trial. Progress has been made, and the care of the children is satisfactory. If the children remain safe, and the improvements are maintained, the NSPCC will recommend to the court that the care orders are revoked.

- Pick out the main events in the case and represent them in a simple flowchart. Here is the start:

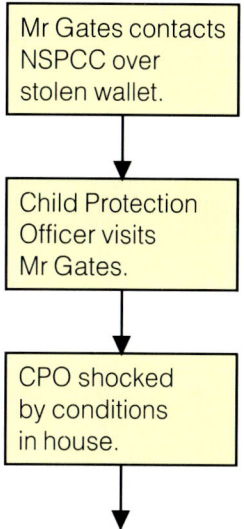

Try to use at least ten boxes. You may use more.

Stage 3 Forming the Pictures

Documentary film-makers often plan their films by first putting together a series of still pictures. This stage is for you to use the pictures or images that form in your mind as you read through the case study, as the basis for your film.

Taking the list you made in Stage 2 turn each box into a picture. Don't worry if you feel you cannot draw. Use stick-figures if you wish. What is important is to have an idea in your mind of what each picture looks like.

Stage 4 Adding the Words

In this stage you have to think about the words spoken in the film.

Add a caption to each of the pictures you have drawn.

They may be something like this:

NSPCC Child Protection Officer arrives.

Child Protection Officer inspects house.

Children's bedroom showing poor conditions.

These captions may be used in your film as part of the commentary.

Documentaries often also use filmed interviews. Write the script of the Child Protection Officer's interview with the family on the following occasions:

a Mr Gates contacts the NSPCC
b Mr Gates reluctantly allows the Child Protection Officer in
c the children are taken into care
d the parents accept they have been at fault
e the children come home for a visit.

You may wish to add a commentary to explain parts of your film that cannot easily be explained by pictures. Sometimes words are spoken as the pictures are shown. These are called **voice-overs**.

Write your own words to be used as voice-overs to explain the following two points:

a the children were neglected, but were suffering as a result of their parents' marital problems;
b the Child Protection Officer worked with the parents to improve the conditions in the house.

Stage 5 The Final Plan

Using the work you have done so far set out your plan for your ten-minute documentary. Some of you may be able to make the film itself.

Here is a suggestion for the beginning:

Shot	Picture	Sound	Time
1	Title of Film: 'We Promise to keep on Caring . . . the work of the NSPCC.'	Music	5 secs.
2		*Commentary* (Voice-over) Mr Gates contacted the NSPCC when he lost his wallet. He had no money to feed his children.	30 secs.
3		*Filmed Interview* CPO: May I speak to you a moment? FATHER: You'd better come in.	60 secs.

BRIEFING

It's in the Script

Here is a page of a script from the soap opera *East Enders*.

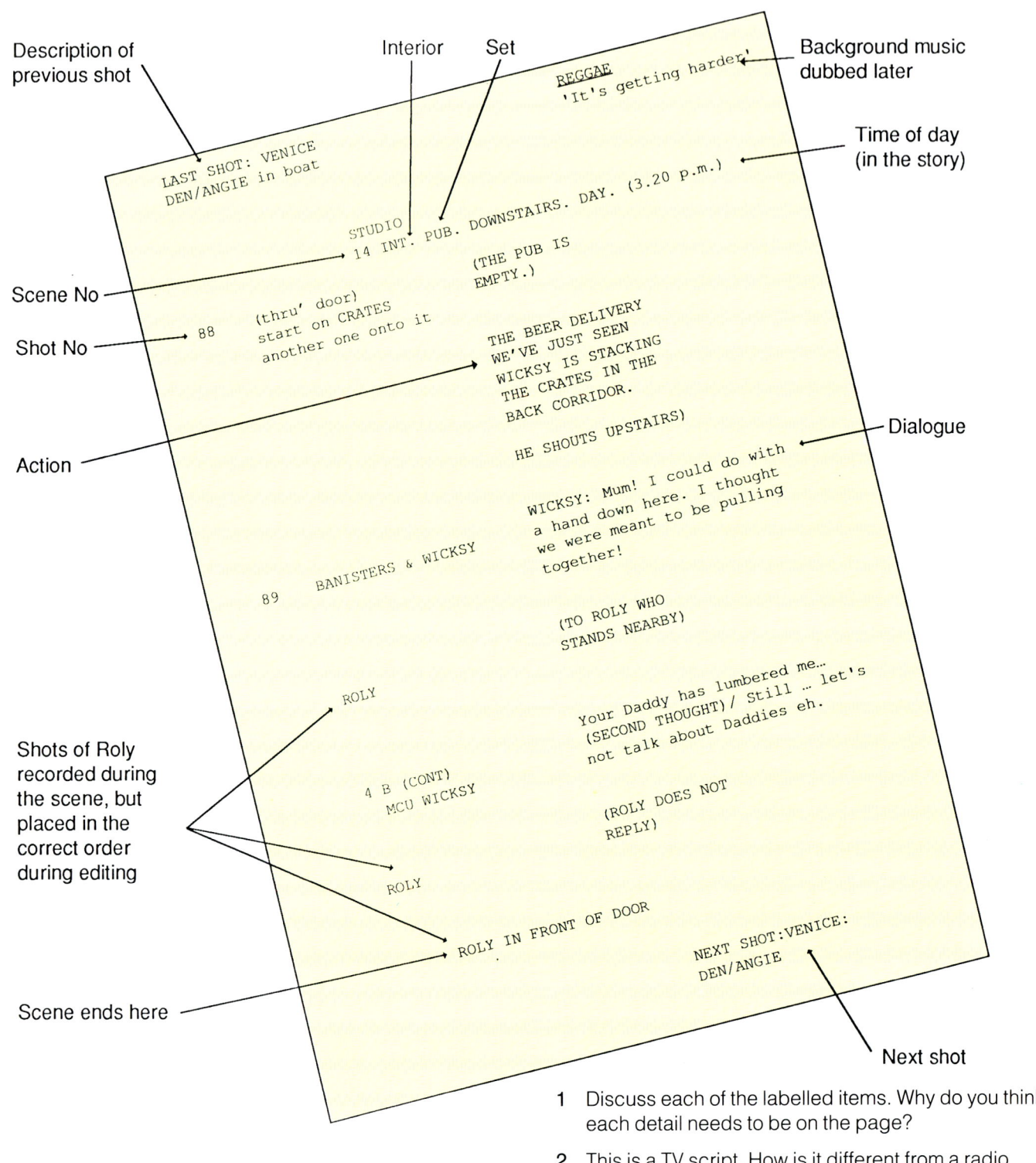

1. Discuss each of the labelled items. Why do you think each detail needs to be on the page?
2. This is a TV script. How is it different from a radio script?

Count Down

Most TV programmes are planned a long time in advance. Soap operas are no exception. Here is the time-table for a typical production of four thirty-minute episodes of a British soap opera.

One Year Ahead:

The Producer and series Script Editor plan the story lines. These show in outline:
- the main events
- the development of the characters in each episode
- the sets
- the number of actors/actresses needed

Every Three Months:

There is a meeting to cover matters brought up by the story line; the need for extra props or cast members; audience reaction and the ratings.

Every Two Weeks:

There is a story-line conference, attended by the Producer, the series Script Editor, the Script Editor and the Scriptwriters for each episode. This conference sorts out details for the next four scripts. When it is over, each writer prepares a short description of his/her episode. This is phoned into the office the next day, typed out and passed on to the Producer and series Script Editor.

After approval, the writer prepares the episode in about two weeks.

The new script is sent to the Script Editor, checked for accuracy, and timed. It is re-typed and a copy is given to all involved in recording the episode.

1 Use this sequence to help you plan a new soap opera.
a Write an outline, or hold a conference in a small group, to decide:
   - the area you will use as background for your soap;
   - the main characters (with a mixture of young and old, to appeal to different viewers);
   - the kinds of stories you will use;
   - the title, opening shots, and credits, to appear each episode.
b Decide the kind of sets and props you will need and sketch one indoor set.
c Plan your first episode. Write a brief description of it and exchange the outline with a partner (or the Script Editor). Discuss possible improvements.
d Write the first few scenes.
e Rehearse; check timing; act out.
f Discuss reactions with your audience and possible ways forward.

Research

Collect more information about jobs in television. You could do this either by writing to, or visiting, your local TV company; inviting a speaker to talk to your group; using library books; taking cuttings from magazines and newspapers. Then present a report on one job, under the headings of:
a Training and qualifications
b Personal qualities needed
c Tasks and responsibilities
d Problems and pleasures

BRIEFING

Writing a Newspaper Article

A newspaper is made up of different sections. The most basic division is between pictures, advertisements and news. Most of the pictures involve people and are linked to news or feature items.

Advertisements may appear in large blocks with illustrations or they may be classified ads. In this case, small amounts of space are bought by people and listed under headings such as For Sale, Births, Deaths, Vacancies.

What is called News includes many items besides simply news reports. For example, there will be:
- overseas news
- local or national news
- sports reports
- features
- editorials
- special columns
- reviews of books, TV, and films

Each of these sections will be written in a different style. There may also be comics, cartoons, crosswords, horoscopes, letters to the editor.

Editorials

The editorial, normally found inside the paper, is written by the editor or another senior writer. It usually comments on an important story or topic. It expresses the opinion of the paper on that topic and often shows the paper's political views.

Features

These are more like the articles you would read in a magazine. Sometimes they are about famous people, discussing their lives or interviewing them or visiting them in their homes. Or they may be about how ordinary people are coping with particular events. Generally, they try to explore a story in greater depth, going 'behind the headlines' to give more detail.

News reports

These try to be brief. They also aim to convey a certain amount of information. They are written in a special way.
a The first sentence is called the *lead* or *intro*. The most important facts appear here in the first paragraph.
b The second sentence gives some more information. Sometimes it is a quotation.
c The next few paragraphs contain more facts which are not so important, or give more details about events. By the end the story has begun to thin out.

News reports are written like this so that they are easy for the sub-editor to cut down to fit the amount of space on a page. The sub-editor will start cutting from the end of the story.

The journalist who writes the story can check it by asking the five W's – Who? What? Where? When? Why? (and sometimes How?). Does the story answer all these questions?

In terms of a diagram the structure of news reports is like a pyramid turned upside down.

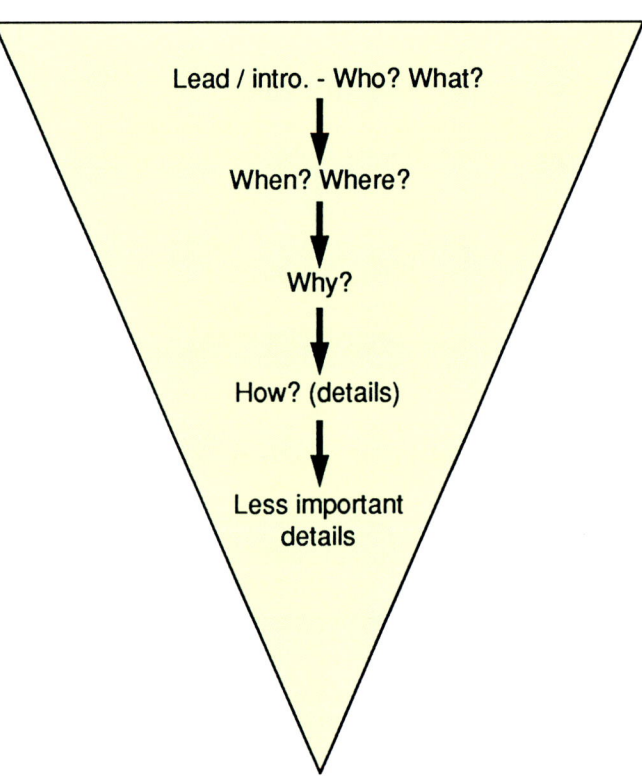

Headlines

Finally, a story will need a headline. Good headlines:
- are in an eye-catching position on the page;
- use lively words to arouse the reader;
- give a clear idea of what is in the story;
- use short snappy words rather than long ones.

Here are three newspaper extracts. Read them carefully and then answer the questions which follow in order to test what you have learned about newspaper writing.

A

Support These Unsung Heroes

WHO SAYS BROWNLOW HAS NO HEART? Once again a quiet hero is about to show us all what real courage is.

Even though he himself suffers from cancer, David Wright is hoping to raise enough money to ensure that more bone marrow transplants take place at the Royal Victoria Hospital.

But does this mean that such fund-raising should be left to the good will of a few brave people! The Echo says No.

Full marks to David Wright and full marks to the hard-working staff of the Royal Vic. But steps must be taken now to ensure that such efforts are backed up by proper financing of hospitals.

Otherwise, the gallant efforts of people like Dave Wright will go to waste.

B

Dave's Sky-Bid To Save Lives.

BROWNLOW cancer victim David Wright wants to make a Jules-Verne style trip to help people who can be saved by transplant operations. At the age of forty-five, the former milkman who cannot have a transplant himself, plans to go around the world in eighty days to help local bone marrow transplant patients.

Backed by Dr Nasima Hussain, hospital consultant, and Captain Roy Waites of British Airways, Mr Wright, of Wood Lane, Brownlow, said, 'This trip will be no joy-ride. I want sponsors who will give hope to suffers all over this area.'

C

June Evans Meets Dave Wright

Wood Lane is an ordinary street in an ordinary part of Brownlow, but there are no ordinary people living at number thirty-two.

For this is the home of Margaret and Dave Wright, a quiet couple who are well known for their fund-raising efforts for the Royal Victoria Hospital's bone marrow transplant unit.

Dave and Margaret are shy people, but their shyness leaves them when they talk about their hopes and fears. Dave has had cancer for two years and talks without bitterness of that time.

'I've no time to feel sorry for myself' he says. 'I want to give something back to that unit which is keeping me alive and give hope to others in this area.'

Margaret nods quietly in agreement, no hint of the anxiety she must feel when she thinks of Dave sky-hiking round the world.

---

1. Of these three pieces from a newspaper, a, b, c, which is the news report, which the feature, and which the editorial? What reasons can you give for the choice you make?

2. Apply the five W questions (Who? What? Where? When? Why?) to the news report. What are the answers?

3. Suggest alternative headlines for those given in a, b, c?

4. All three extracts have some of the same details, but each extract has details which are not found in the other two. What are those details in a, b, and c?

5. Write short snappy headlines for these stories:
   - A father and son team are hoping to make a pop record.
   - A TV personality wants to stop a health farm being opened near a small village.
   - A former magistrate has been convicted of a drinking offence.
   - A sudden thaw has caused problems on local main roads.
   - A local football manager has money to spend on new players.
   - A young bride has made a miraculous recovery after being injured in a car crash.

6. Cut out three news reports from local or national newspapers. Apply the five W questions (Who? What? Where? When? Why? and How?) and underline the answers with coloured pen.

Research

After looking at several different kinds of paper, use the knowledge you have gained from this Unit to write a newspaper report or editorial or feature. This could be on:
- a real happening in your own experience
- an invented incident
- an important topic that interests you

BRIEFING

Film Reviews

These two reviews of *Rambo III* are taken from very different sources, intended for different audiences, but they are written in a very similar way. The notes show you *the form* of the two reviews.

Rambo III (18)

Blimey, if it isn't the old meathead himself, Sylvester Stallone, brought out of 're-tirement' to save the world from lousy, rotten, slimey, 'commies' yet again. The scene of the carnage this time is Afghanistan where his old pal Colonel Trautman is being held prisoner, and getting knocked about something horrible by those nasty Russians in a so-called unassailable mountain top fortress. Needless to say what follows is a non-stop action-packed caper full of heroics as Rambo equipped with every piece of high-tech weaponry, including a bow and arrow which shoots down helicopters, blasts his way in and out of the fortress, gets chased all over and, er, under the Afghan countryside, despatches an evil Ruskie approximately every two milliseconds, utters immortal lines of dialogue i.e. 'uh-huh' and 'yeah', and wrestles tanks with his bare hands (well almost). Of course it's all very predictable and thus somewhat lacking in any kind of suspense or drama. Perfect for those who loved *Rambo I&II* but not much cop for those who didn't.

Graeme Kay
Smash Hits

- Opening witty or striking comment to catch reader's attention
- The setting - where the action takes place
- Starting point for the plot - what the film is about
- Reviewer's comment on the action
- Highlighting memorable details from the film
- Reviewer's personal opinion - assessment of the film as a whole

---

THE first utterance made by Sylvester Stallone in **Rambo III** (Odeon West End, 18) is 'I don't believe this,' and in the ensuing hour and a half the spectator has ample opportunities to echo his words.

This time round Rambo, is first discovered living as odd job man at a Buddhist monastery. When his old CO (Richard Crenna) seeks to enlist him for an undercover sortie into Afghanistan (the actual purpose of which never becomes any too clear), Rambo turns him down. But when word arrives that Crenna has fallen into the clutches of the Ruskies, our hero wastes no time in saddling up for a virtually one-man rescue mission.

The action takes a long time to get going. Once it arrives, there is no shortage of deafening sound and fury, but not much in the way of suspense, even at the crudest blood-and-thunder level.

The reason for this seems to be two-fold. For one thing, Rambo's indestructibility is akin to that of a cartoon cat, which after being blown to smithereens in one shot can magically reassemble itself for the next. In Rambo's case, it is true, this may entail a spot of amateur surgery on himself, manifested in a scene (during which this viewer's eyes remained tightly shut) of his digging a bullet out of himself, with apparently no after-effects lasting more than a few minutes.

The final sequence of the escape to the frontier escalates into wilder and wilder fantasy such as to bludgeon disbelief into a state of suspension, but it proves too little too late. The film ends, incidentally, with a dedication to 'the gallant people of Afghanistan'. One hesitates to speculate upon what their reaction to this rather curious tribute might be.

Tim Pullein
The Guardian

Here, now, are different reviews of another film *Wall Street*. One is taken from *Smash Hits*, a magazine aimed primarily at British teenagers and devoted to pop stars and music. The other is from *The New Internationalist*, a magazine with a worldwide distribution which reports on issues of world poverty and inequality.

Read the reviews and answer the questions which follow.

Wall Street
directed by Oliver Stone

Movies have a head start when they tackle war and repression in some exotic location as Oliver Stone did with his first two features, *Platoon* and *Salvado*.

Enthralling a viewer with the sight of men in pin-stripe suits staring at computer screens or talking about company balance sheets is rather more difficult.

That Stone pulls it off is partly because of his own sharp script and partly because we cannot help but be aware that these concrete canyons of Manhattan harbour even more power than the military forces of the previous films.

This is a simple morality play: a young innocent is drawn into corruption.

Ultimately he comes to his senses - though not in time to avert a fall. We ride with Buddy up through the frantic wheeler-dealing and share his fascination with Gordon Gekko, the ruthless asset stripper who grooms him for the penthouse. Michael Douglas won an Oscar for playing Gekko though, as usual, it was the acting part as much as the acting which was rewarded. Gekko is both the incarnation of Market Man and the reincarnation of a Medieval Deadly Sin. 'Greed is right, greed is good,' he says. 'It's all about bucks - the rest is conservation': 'if you need a friend get a dog - it's trench warfare out there'.

Stone continues to make radical films that reach a mass audience through the force of his wit, style and popular appeal. Where else in Hollywood would you hear the observation that the richest one per cent in the US owns half the wealth? More power to his heart.

Politics ☆☆☆☆
Entertainment ☆☆☆☆

The New Internationalist

WALL STREET (15)

A film about The New York Stock Exchange sounds about as exciting as a new Shakin' Stevens LP but in fact *Wall Street* is an engrossing peek into the terrifying world of high finance where millions of dollars are bandied about as casually as bingo numbers and ulcers are as common as 'flu. Charlie Sheen plays clean-cut and slightly gonky Bud (Ugh! *Why* do they always have such *horrible* names?) Fox, a broker working in this stomach-churningly frantic environment, who is desperate to make a pile of cash and his reputation as a sharp wheeler-dealer. He engineers his way under the wing of a sun-tanned, sharp-suited and totally lethal businessman, Gordon Gekko (superbly played by Michael Douglas) a man with a nice line in greased back hair and seriously loadsa money. A couple of dodgy deals later, Bud swaps his bedsit for a glass-walled penthouse, acquires a set of designer threads and another perk of having pots of loot is his girlfriend interior designer Darien (Daryl Hannah). But of course, there is a price to pay. *Wall Street* is set in some pretty swanky - and apparently genuine - locations, there's a good soundtrack by Talking Heads and even if you don't know what a share index is (or you don't particularly care) it's still absolutely enthralling.

Smash Hits

1. What is the first point that each reviewer makes?
2. What does each reviewer tell us about the action of the film?
3. What comments does each reviewer make about the performances of the actors?
4. Give one piece of information (not opinion) from each review which is not included in the other.
5. A friend says to you, 'All this review business is rubbish. *Rambo* is about killing and *Wall Street* is about greed. That's what people really want.' Judging by these four reviews, tell your friend whether such films as these do good or do harm.

Research

Write a review of a film you know well, trying to follow the sequence shown in the two *Rambo* reviews. Ask your partner to pick out the six sections and to say how successful you have been in explaining the film clearly.

Here is a selection of previews advertising some of the films shown on ITV during one Christmas.
Trying not to allow your own knowledge of the films to influence you, say, from these descriptions, which of them you would be tempted to watch.

The Ugly Dachshund

Flimsy Disney whimsy about a filthy-rich young couple who adopt a Great Dane puppy as a brother for their four dachshund bitches. 'You've got a boy puppy,' he tells his wife. 'That's what you always wanted.' Dean Jones and Suzanne Pleshette coat the treacle. *1965*

Murder by Decree

Sherlock Holmes meets Jack the Ripper again. Despite a stellar cast, the real star of this gaslit chiller is production designer Harry Pottle, who creates narrow, grimy streets, vaguely welcoming taverns, gaunt wharves and battered Victorian slums with all the flair of the old Hollywood. The film itself does its job well as a baffling thriller until the superfluous last half-hour. Christopher Plummer is the caped super-sleuth, and James Mason excellent as Dr Watson. *1978*

Lord of the Rings

Director Ralph Bakshi's attempt to set down an animated version of J R R Tolkien's massive saga of Middle Earth (or at least the first half of it) must go down as a jolly good try at an almost impossible project. Certain sections – the mines of Moria; the Ringwraiths in the sky – are bitingly close to one's visualisation of the book. *1978*

Shane

Once-and-for-all embodiment of the finest in westerns, about the gunman from nowhere, looking for peace but finding only another fight. The gunplay is magnetically powerful and the camerawork superb. *Shane* totally revived Alan Ladd's career, in a role similar to the one that originally shot him to stardom in *This Gun for Hire* *1953*

The Hound of the Baskervilles

'There are many things on the moor that are not what they seem,' mutters Glynis Barber. And how right she is, in this seventh film version (and about the only one not yet seen on TV) of the Conan Doyle Sherlock Holmes classic. Douglas Hickox films it as a proper Victorian melodrama, full of ominous close-ups of people looking suspicious. 'It was fear that killed him, Mr Holmes,' says another character. 'Fear.' That, perhaps and a close look at the script.

The Empire Strikes Back

Long-awaited television premiere of the second in the *Star Wars* trilogy. A masterpiece of special effects, it punctuates a tortuous storyline with bursts of swift and violent action.

1980

Gremlins

Basically a children's film with horrific overtones, this is a vastly entertaining fantasy, directed by Joe (*Innerspace*) Dante, who doesn't miss a trick from the moody opening in Chinatown when Papa (Hoyt Axton, whose narration and performance are both spot-on) buys a Mugwai there. The highlight of the fun and games is undoubtedly the ingenious scene in which Axton's wife disposes of several death-bent gremlins with various kitchen contrivances.

1984

The Little Match Girl

Hans Christian Andersen's sad fairy tale survives this Americanised update, with Keshia Knight Pulliam (the tiny tot star of *The Cosby Show*) as a homeless orphan who brings light into people's lives. Polished playing by William Daniels and Rue McClanahan suits the sumptuous production but there are rather too many wobbly 'Oirish' accents dished out by the downstairs kitchen staff.

TVM 1987

The Snowman

Without doubt one of the finest and most influential British animated films of recent times, made by the same company that produced that distinctive Beatles cartoon *Yellow Submarine*.

TVM 1982

1. If you were asked to put the films into rank order, which would be your top two and bottom two for family Christmas viewing? For what reasons?
2. Explain how the writer's own likes and dislikes are shown in these pieces.

Research

Write previews of two films which you think would make good family viewing over a holiday period. Try to imitate the style of the *TV Times* previews, in terms of:
- length
- references to plot/action/actors
- fairly strong final sentence

Glossary

animation bringing puppets or drawings to life for cartoons and films.

appeal what makes a media product – such as an advertisement, TV programme, film, newspaper, pop record, magazine – attractive to a particular audience.

audience the group of people that a media product is especially aimed at. The group could be chosen on the basis of age, sex, income.

autocue a device which shows the presenter's script in front of the camera lens.

bias the way a programme or piece of writing is slanted to support a particular point of view.

brand image the feelings and thoughts which are associated with a particular product.

broadsheet newspapers which appear in a large format (for example *The Times, The Daily Telegraph, The Independent, The Guardian*).

cable TV a system for transmitting any number of TV channels to subscribers on the cable network (similar to telephone cable) which allows users both to receive and to send signals. (For example, to shop or bank via TV.)

camera angles the position of the camera in relation to the subject being photographed, such as big close up (eg a head); long shot (eg person plus scenery); wide angle (gives the maximum view); high angle (the camera looks down on the subject).

caption the words in small type which explain details in a photograph.

circulation the number of copies a paper or magazine sells.

commentator a person who talks about an event (often sporting) as it is happening to explain it to viewers.

commercial a radio or TV advertisement.

coverage the reporting of an event by newspapers and other media.

cover lines short written summaries alongside a photograph or cartoon.

cropping the cutting of a photograph to improve it or change its message.

deadline the date by which an article or programme must be ready for the editor.

director the person responsible in film/TV/theatre for bringing a script to life, supervising the technicians and rehearsing the artistes.

editorial a newspaper article which puts forward the opinion of the editor or leader-writer.

feature a special article in a newspaper or magazine which treats a topic in greater depth than a news story.

freelance a person who is not under contract to one company but is free to offer work (eg film/articles/art/photographs) to any company.

galley proof an early example of a page, made before printing, in order to correct errors.

genre a kind or type. In the media certain types of films, radio and television programmes can be grouped together because they are of the same genre. They will share some characteristics. For example, most crime series will have policemen, criminals, guns, fast cars. Other TV genres are: soap opera; situation comedy; documentary; game show.

identification the way people link themselves with (and even see themselves as the same as) a character in a book, film or play; or associate themselves with a particular newspaper or magazine.

image something made by one person to be looked at by another, eg photo, drawing, TV still.

image the ideas and feelings which are aroused by a particular advert, film, photo, or even a person (eg a pop star may have a rebel image; *Coca Cola* may present an outdoor, sporty, youthful, image).

location the place where filming occurs (Int. = interior, Ext. = exterior).

logo the design used to promote a product or a company, so that when we see the logo, we automatically think of what it stands for.

market research the way in which companies use questionnaires and samples of opinion to find out what people want and what they feel about products (including TV/radio programmes).

mass media the means of communicating with very large numbers of people, eg through advertising; newspapers and magazines; film; TV and radio; pop music.

narrative telling the story; the selection and order of events and the way they unfold in a film, advert, book, documentary, news broadcast.

news report a description in a newspaper of a very recent event. News reports have a particular structure.

novelisation a real event is used as the basis for a book. However good the research, the writer will have to re-create many scenes in words. Thus, a novelisation is not completely fact nor fiction, but something in between.

presenter a person who gives information to TV viewers or radio listeners (eg a news-reader) or is on screen in charge of certain TV programmes (eg *Panorama*, chat shows etc.).

press release a statement given to the media by a government department or large company or official.

producer the person responsible for all aspects of a film/TV/radio programme/play. He/she commissions a script; appoints the director; decides on timetable and budget; makes most of the major decisions.

promotion all the ways in which a product (including a film or book) is advertised. In the case of a film, this might be by interviews with the stars; clips on TV; trailers at the cinema; reviews in newspapers or magazines; adverts; posters.

representation the way certain groups in society are presented by the media.

reviews a report on TV, radio or in the press which describes or criticises a recent film, book, programme, or other event.

satellite TV the means by which TV programmes can be transmitted to many countries. A ground station 'uplinks' the signal to the satellite. The satellite 'downlinks' the signal to a satellite dish. A decoder in the TV unscrambles the signal and gives the picture.

schedule a list of items. On TV this will be a list of programmes. In publishing it will be a list of articles, their lengths and deadlines for completion.

scheduling the time, day and order in which TV programmes are transmitted. A schedule is planned in order to attract particular audiences, bearing in mind the competition.

situation comedy (sitcom) a humorous TV or radio series which depends on a particular location and set of characters.

soap opera a long-running TV or radio drama series telling of the lives and loves of a group of people in a particular location (eg *Dallas, The Archers, Neighbours, East Enders*).

stereotype originally a printing plate that was used many times. Now the word refers to the way an image or belief is used unthinkingly about a single person or a whole group of people.

story-board in film or TV, a detailed sketch of a camera shot or series of shots, usually with a brief description.

story-line the brief outline of what will happen in a film/interview/TV programme.

sub-editing the way an editor or sub-editor will cut, correct, or alter an article before it is published.

tabloid a newspaper which is half the size of the broadsheet newspapers. Tabloids use a lot of pictures, large headlines, and brief reports. Examples are: *The Daily Mirror, The Daily Express, The Daily Mail, The Sun, Today*.

targeting aiming a film/magazine/TV/radio programme/advert at a particular group of people.

teletext brief written items of information shown on TV screens through systems such as Oracle or Ceefax.

voice-over (V.O.) the background commentary which accompanies a film or TV commercial.

Skills Checklist for Teachers

An indication is given for many of the listed skills of the Attainment Targets (AT) and Levels (L) to which they may correspond, in terms of the National Curriculum. Some skills overlap; some are capable of interpretation across a wide range.
AT1 = Speaking and Listening
AT2 = Reading
AT3 = Writing

Writing Skills

1. Variety of form, i.e. advertisement; biography; caption; checklist; evaluation; film script; heading; instruction; leaflet; letter; log; magazine and newspaper article; matrix; memo; photo-story; play and TV script; poem; questionnaire; report; review; scrapbook; script for advert, TV and radio; short story; slogan; story-board; survey; synopsis; teletext. (AT3: L 5, 6, 7, 8, 9, 10)
2. Opportunity for personal, narrative and reflective writing and for the language of argument, conversation, description, explanation and persuasion. (AT3: L 5, 6, 7, 8, 9, 10)
3. Advice on the processes of writing, including drafting. (AT3: L 4, 5, 6, 7)
4. Consideration of audience and purposes for writing. (AT3: L 5, 6, 7, 8, 9, 10)
5. Advice on planning and presenting an advertisement, documentary, magazine and newspaper article, review, script. (AT3: L 9)
6. Invention of a language, with translation. (AT2: L 9)
7. Appreciation of sequencing. (AT3: L 4, 5, 6, 7, 8, 9, 10)
8. Interpretation of character and actions. (AT2: L 5, 6, 7, 8, 9, 10)
9. Translation of written information into visual form, and vice-versa. (AT3: L 6, 8)
10. Transformation from one genre into another. (AT3: L 7, 9)

Reading Skills

1. Interpretation of material in a variety of written forms and genres (including charts; film scripts; reviews; pamphlets; magazine extracts; transcripts) and from world sources. (AT2: L 7, 8, 9, 10)
2. Practice of intermediate and higher reading skills, such as: comprehension; prediction; inferential understanding. (AT2: L 7, 8, 9, 10)
3. Identification of stereotypes. (AT2: L 9)
4. Appreciation of tone, content and form, language and visual conventions. (AT2: L 7, 8, 9)
5. Response to a range of fiction and factual material. (AT2: L 4, 5, 6, 7, 8, 9, 10)
6. Practice in reading aloud. (AT1: L 5, 6)
7. Selection of information and scrutiny of text. (AT2: L 4, 5, 6, 7, 8, 9, 10)
8. Personal research and study skills. (AT2: L 6, 7, 8, 9, 10)
9. Development of powers of discrimination, particularly in context of advertising material, and between facts and theories. (AT2: L 5, 6, 7, 8, 9, 10)

Visual Awareness

1. Analysis of TV news presentation.
2. Awareness of camera angles.
3. Comparison of writing with graphic presentation.
4. Consideration of comic conventions.
5. Development of perspectives and points of view.
6. Interpretation of posters.
7. Invitation to use a variety of media hardware and software
8. Linking of written commentary with photographs.
9. Scrutiny of a range of images of visual material.

Oral Skills

1. Advice on, and opportunity for, debate, set talks, small group discussion and one-to-one language work. (AT1: L 4,5,7,8)
2. Variety of simulation activities and opportunity for role play and improvisation in small group drama. (AT1: L 6)
3. Response to visual and diagrammatic material. (AT2: L 5)
4. Use of language to converse, explain, explore, interpret, persuade. (AT1: L 6)
5. Opportunities for interviewing and tape-recording and scrutiny of video extracts. (AT1: L 9)
6. Analysis of spoken language in different contexts and by different media, and of the differences between spoken and written language. (AT1: L 7. AT3: L 6, 8)
7. Preparation of, and support for, a case. (AT1: L 5, 7, 9, 10)
8. Regular practice in exercising choices. AT1: L 8, 9)

Concepts/Knowledge

1. Construction of a range of media products.
2. Developments in cable/satellite TV.
3. Individual companies, real people, and their work.
4. Jobs in the media industry.
5. Key concepts such as: appeal; audience; genre; identification; image; marketing; representation; stereotyping; targeting.
6. Narrative and special effects in film.
7. Regulation and control of advertising and the media.
8. Role of the interviewer.
9. Structure and form of media artefacts.

Attitudes

1. Exercise of choice and responsibility for making judgements.
2. Extension of empathy in a variety of contexts but particularly in relation to those in difficulty.
3. Critical approach towards the mass media.
4. Extension of multi-cultural awareness and understanding.
5. Opportunity to measure real experience against that of others (both in real life and via fiction).
6. Practice at prioritising.
7. Representation of groups in the media.
8. Exploration of variety of moral stances and current issues, such as: care of young children; conflict; corporate power; environment; future; human rights; influence and responsibility; intrusive photography; justice; love; manipulation of individuals; mass media; sex roles; standards and taste; television violence.

Note The Research suggestions made in the Units generally depend on material outside the classroom. Many of them have specifically been designed for G.C.S.E. English and G.C.S.E. Media Studies project work.

ACKNOWLEDGEMENTS

The Editors and Publishers gratefully acknowledge permission to reprint the following copyright material.

Advertising
David Ogilvy: from *Ogilvy on Advertising*, (Orbis, 1983), by permission of Multimedia Books Limited, London. Extracts from *The Financial Times*, 20 Feb. 1988, with their permission. Extracts from article by Dudley Doust: *The Sunday Times*, 21 Feb. 1988, © Times Newspapers Limited 1988, by permission of Times Newspapers Ltd. Extracts from *Today*, BBC Radio 4, 19 Feb. 1988, by permission of the British Broadcasting Corporation.

Television and radio
Chris Miller and Gill Stribling-Wright: from *Cilla Black's Blind Date*, (Dregon, 1987), © LWT 1987, by permission of Collins Publishers. Laurie Taylor and Bob Mullan: from *Uninvited Guests*, (Chatto & Windus, 1986), by permission of the publishers on behalf of the authors. Extracts from *Putting Women in the Picture*, BBC 1, 24 August 1987, and *Network*, BBC 1, 7 June 1988, by permission of the British Broadcasting Corporation. Extracts from *Right to Reply*, by permission of the author. Extract from *The Radio Times*, by permission of BBC Enterprises. Extract from *Jackie*, © D.C. Thomson & Co Ltd, by permission of D.C. Thomson. Extract from *Today*, BBC Radio 4, 19 November 1987, by permission of the British Broadcasting Corporation. M. Marland and R. Willcox (Editors) for extract from *While They Fought*, (Longman, 1980), by permission of the publishers.

Newspapers
Extracts from *Today*, BBC Radio 4, 19 November 1987, by permission of the British Broadcasting Corporation of the interviewees. Bob Geldof, for extract from *Is That It?*, (Sidgwick & Jackson, 1986), by permission of the publishers. Extract from *Oxfam News*, by permission of Oxfam. Book jacket for *The Killing of Karen Silkwood*, by Richard Raschke, (Sphere, 1983), by permission of Sphere Books Limited. Extracts from *The Science Show*, ABC Radio 2, 17 April 1979, by permission of Australian Broadcasting Corporation. Howard John: *Who Killed Karen Silkwood?*, (Summit, 1981) by permission of Howard John.

Magazines and comics
Extract from *The Radio Times*, by permission of BBC Enterprises. Extracts from *Atari ST User*, June 1988, by permission of the Editor. Extract from *Weekend*, November 1985, by permission of Associated Magazines Ltd. Extract from *Which?*, April 1987, by permission of the Consumers' Association. Extract from *Blue Jeans*, © D.C. Thomson & Co Ltd, by permission of the Editor and IPC Magazines. Front cover of *The Jewish Chronicle, Colour Magazine*, reproduced by permission of Gerald Jacobs, Editor. Robert Sandall for 'How to make a song and dance of a pop concert', in *The Sunday Times*, 17 July 1988, © Times Newspapers Limited 1988, by permission of Times Newspapers Ltd. Adam Sweeting for article in *The Guardian*, 16 July 1988, by permission of the author. Annette Witheridge for article in *The Star*, 17 May 1988, by permission of Express Newspapers Plc. Sylvia Petterson for reviews in *Smash Hits*, August/September 1987, by permission of EMAP/Metro Publications Ltd. Extracts from advice leaflet published by D.C. Thomson & Co Ltd, © D.C. Thomson & Co Ltd, by permission of the publishers. Eileen McCauley: 'The Seduction', winner of The Observer Poetry Competition, 1987, © *The Observer*, by permission of The Observer Ltd. Raymond Briggs for extract from *Where the Wind Blows*, (Hamish Hamilton, 1982), by permission of the publishers.

Film
Extracts from the Educational Mail section of *The Courier-Mail*, (Brisbane, 1982), by permission of The Courier-Mail. John Boorman: *Hope and Glory - The Screenplay*, (Faber, 1987), and John Ford and Dudley Nicholls: *Stagecoach* (screenplay), Classic Film Script, 1984, by permission of Faber and Faber Ltd. Fareth Owen for extract from *Song of the City*, (Fontana, 1985) by permission of Collins, Publishers. Ann Lloyd (Editor) for extract from *Movies of the Seventies*, (Orbis, 1984), by permission of MacDonald and Co (Publishers) Ltd. Andrew Langley for extract from *The Making of the Living Planet*, (Allen & Unwin, in association with Absolute Press, 1985), by permission of Unwin Hyman Ltd. Extracts from *Return of the Jedi*, (Paradise Press, 1983), © and TM 1983 Lucasfilm Ltd., by permission of Lucasfilm Ltd.

Briefing
Table from *Advertising*, by Michael Pollard, (Penguin Books, 1988) copyright © Michael Pollard, 1988, by permission of the publishers. Table from *The Last Picture Show*, by D. Docherty, D. Morrison and M. Tracey, (B.F.I., 1987), by permission of the Broadcasting Research Unit. Advertising Standards Authority advertisement by permission of the ASA Ltd. Material from NSPCC leaflets, by permission of the NSPCC. Extract from *Eastenders*, BBC TV Speical, (Grandreams, 1987), by permission of the publishers. Tim Pulleine for article in *The Guardian*, 25 August 1988, by permission of the author. Graeme Kay for article in *Smash Hits*, August 1988 and film review, *Smash Hits*, April 1988, by permission of EMAP/Metro Publications Ltd. Film review, *New Internationalist*, July 1988, by permission of New Internationalist. Reviews from *TV Times*, by permission of Independent Television Publications Ltd.

The Author p.4/5; Courtesy of National Savings p.6; Popperfoto p.8/9; The Guardian p.11, 27; Courtesy of Gold, Greenless, Trott p.12/13; Courtesy of LWT p.17/18; Channel Four p.20 (top); Granada Television p.20 (bottom); Central Independent Television p.22/23; Nils Jorgensen/Rex Features p.39/40; Photographer/Rex Features p. 48, 59; Wendy Wallace p.49; Kobal Collection p.64, 71, 76/77, 79/80, 84; National Film Archive, London p.68; Poster of Willow unknown, others National Film Archive, London p.69; Lucasfilm Ltd. p.85; J. Allan Cash p.86 (top); Barnaby's Picture Library p.86 (bottom). John Walmsley p.16 (top and third from top), 17 (second from top), 27, 47 (all), 94 (top left).

Illustrations are by Martin Chatterton, Chris Duggan, Martin Eastcott, Martin Hargreaves, John Ireland, Peter Joyce, Chris Price and Laura Roberts.

Although every effort has been made to trace and contact copyright owners, we have not been successful in a few cases. We apologise for any infringement of copyright, and will be pleased to rectify the matter at the earliest opportunity.

The following material appears for the first time in this publication:
'Famine' by Zoe Guest, with thanks. 'Children at the Gate', with thanks to the children and to David Calcutt.